The Olympic Games

The Olympic Games

Look for these and other books in the Lucent Overview Series:

Advertising
The Collapse of the Soviet Union
Drug Abuse
Drugs and Sports
The Reunification of Germany
Sports in America
The United Nations
Women's Rights

The Olympic Games

by Stephen Currie

LUCENT
BOOKS

LUCENT *Overview Series*

LUCENT *Overview Series*

Library of Congress Cataloging-in-Publication Data

Currie, Stephen, 1960–
    The Olympic games / by Stephen Currie.
       p. cm. — (Lucent overview series)
    Includes bibliographical references (p.) and index.
    Summary: Discusses various aspects of the Olympic games,
including their history, politics, commercialization, size,
participation, and drug use.
    ISBN 1-56006-395-5 (lib. bdg.)
    1. Olympics—History—Juvenile literature. 2. Olympics—Social
aspects—Juvenile literature. [1. Olympics.] I. Title. II. Series.
  GV721.5.C87   1999
  796.48'09—dc21
                                            98-50360
                                               CIP
                                               AC

Copyright © 1999 by Lucent Books, Inc.
P.O. Box 289011, San Diego, CA 92198-9011
Printed in the U.S.A.

Contents

Introduction

THE ORIGINAL OLYMPIC Games were an invention of the ancient Greeks. There are no clear records of exactly when and where the first Games took place, though some experts believe they may date back to 1300 B.C.E. We are certain, however, that an athletic competition identified as "Olympic" took place in the year 776 B.C.E. By modern standards, these Games were very limited. They may have consisted of only one event: a sprint. There were no team sports, no stadium lighting, and no uniforms: indeed, the athletes competed nude.

The early Olympics also had no women. The Greeks considered the Games to be the specific preserve of men, mainly because they intended sports to mirror war and to prepare participants for battle. Indeed, the Greeks took great pains to keep the Games an all-male affair. The ancient Olympics were closed not only to female competitors but also to female spectators. Any who sneaked in were put to death.

From this small start, however, the Olympics grew. Held every four years, regardless of war, illness, or famine, they continued far longer than any of the original competitors could have imagined. Events were added one by one to the program: wrestling and jumping, boxing and the discus, distance running and the javelin. The Games lasted through the fall of Greece and the rise of imperial Rome. They were finally stopped in the fourth century C.E. by the Roman emperor Theodosius. A Christian, Theodosius objected to the pagan aspects of the custom: Mount Olympus

Greek athletes compete in the Olympic Games. Unlike the modern Olympics, these ancient games were reserved for men, and athletes competed in the nude.

was believed to be the home of the many deities traditionally worshiped in Greece.

After more than a thousand years, then, the Games were at an end. Then in the early nineteenth century the idea of recreating a modern Olympics took hold. The most influential proponent of a revival was a French baron named Pierre de Coubertin. In 1892 Coubertin formally proposed holding a series of games every four years, games to which the whole world would be invited. In his opinion, these new Olympics would not only give young athletes a chance to compete against each other, but they would carry moral value as well. The athletic competition, he believed, would be a wonderful way to bring the nations of the world together in a peaceful gathering.

The first modern Games took place in Athens, Greece, during the spring of 1896. By current standards both the organization and the athleticism were poor. Swimming races were held in the choppy, cold Sea of Crete, which lies between the Mediterranean Sea and the Aegean. One competitor dived into the water and immediately jumped out, complaining that he was freezing. There were arguments over the proper rules for several sports, notably gymnastics. A few medals went to athletes with little experience in their sports. The world's athletes and governments took little notice of the Games, and the world's press showed even less interest.

French educator and sports enthusiast Baron Pierre de Coubertin is credited with the revival of the Olympic Games. His dream of a world-wide Olympic competition was realized when the modern Games were held in Athens in 1896.

Beyond 1896

But the Games were successful enough to allow Coubertin to continue. The 1900 Olympics occurred as scheduled, in Paris, and attracted a few more competitors from a few more nations. The 1904 St. Louis Games also went on as planned. Both Olympics, though, were attached to world's fairs and did not get the publicity the promoters had hoped for. The first Olympics to make a serious impact, then, were the 1908 Games in London, England. With over two thousand competitors and a stadium that held a hundred thousand fans, the Olympics were established at last.

The Games continue today. Now, though, they are wildly popular. Tickets to some competitions sell out almost as soon as they are put on sale. No regularly scheduled event is watched more widely on television; some observers estimate that half the population of the entire world saw at least some of the 1996 Atlanta Games. The Olympics bring obscure sports and athletes into the world's living rooms, causing even nonfans to suddenly care about women's gymnastics, the men's giant slalom, or the 100-meter backstroke.

Yet the Olympics have had a rocky history. They have been plagued with controversy since the start. Questions of who should be allowed to compete appeared as early as 1896. Other thorny problems soon emerged as well. At times it has seemed that the Olympic movement was about to fall apart under its own weight. In fact, from time to time people have suggested that the world would be a better place if it did. The Games have been accused of compromising sportsmanship, inflaming political passions, and establishing an atmosphere in which cheating is rewarded.

These controversies, whether arguments over the participation of professionals, the role of commercial funding, or the menace of steroids, are fundamentally questions about the proper direction for the Olympics. It was not inevitable that the Games should be the size they are today, that they should admit athletes from every country, or even that they should exist at all. The Games are what they are today because of the issues that have arisen in the past and because of the way in which officials, fans, and athletes have reacted to those issues. In the future, the Games will continue to be shaped by the controversies that surround them. What they will look like in 2008 or 2064 is anybody's guess. Nevertheless, an understanding of the forces that have shaped them in the past will be helpful to understanding how other forces may affect them in the future.

1

Professionals and Amateurs

In 1950 THE Associated Press asked journalists to name the greatest athlete of the first half of the twentieth century. For most voters, the choice was easy. Bypassing a host of swimmers, football players, and cyclists, along with such big names as baseball player Babe Ruth, the Associated Press's membership selected Jim Thorpe. A Native American who grew up in Oklahoma, Thorpe was an athletic prodigy. As a student at Carlisle University he played eleven different varsity sports; he was also the winner of the 1912 college ballroom dancing championship. Though he never made it big in professional team sports, Thorpe's extraordinary ability in so many different sports made him an outstanding athlete indeed.

Nowhere was Thorpe's ability greater than in track and field. In 1912 his foot speed and jumping ability won him a berth on the U.S. team bound for the Stockholm Olympics. Thorpe performed magnificently at the Games. He won the decathlon, a competition involving ten different track and field events. His score of 8412 smashed the world record by almost a thousand points. Thorpe also was the pentathlon champion, and he won medals in the high jump and long jump competitions. Almost overnight, he was an international hero. King Gustav V of Sweden called him the "greatest athlete in the world."[1] The Russian czar presented him with a gold-plated chalice. Back home in the United States, Thorpe was given a ticker-tape parade.

But the glory did not last. Early in 1913 the U.S. and International Olympic Committees ruled that Thorpe had been ineligible to compete in the 1912 Games. They asserted that he had violated Rule 26 of the International Olympic Committee (IOC) charter, which required that athletes be amateurs—that is, that they receive no pay for their performances. Technically, the charge was accurate: needing to support himself between college semesters, Thorpe had played minor league baseball during the summers of 1909 and 1910. He had earned $25 a week. Still, even that small sum made him a professional athlete, who was therefore ineligible to compete in the Olympics. Thorpe's medals were taken away, and his name was removed from the Olympic record books.

Over the years, however, more and more people became convinced that the IOC had acted unfairly. Not only had Thorpe earned very little money for his athletic ability, but he had earned it in a sport—baseball—very different from the track and field events in which he had competed. At last, in 1982, nearly thirty years after Thorpe's death, the IOC took action. It voted to restore Thorpe's name to the record books. The following January, his medals were presented to his children.

Legendary athlete Jim Thorpe (second from left) participates in the 1,500-meter race during the 1912 Olympic Games. Thorpe, who won numerous medals at the 1912 Games, was stripped of them after the IOC learned that the star athlete was not a full-fledged amateur.

Amateurs and professionals

The question of amateurism has never ceased to plague the modern Olympics. While Jim Thorpe is among only a very few competitors to be banned after the fact for professionalism, many more athletes have been denied entry for related reasons. Thorpe's story plays up the unwillingness of many early Olympic administrators to allow the entry of professionals into the Games—an unwillingness that has not been completely resolved even today.

For Baron de Coubertin, the founder of the modern Olympics, amateur athletics were far superior to professional athletics. Coubertin, and many others of his time, drew a sharp distinction between the goals and methods of amateur and professional athletes. Amateur athletes, Coubertin pointed out, did not depend on their sport to earn a living. Thus, they were more likely to play fair, to be good sports, and to appreciate their opponents' abilities.

Professional sports, in contrast, were considered rough and mean, and the competitors were believed to be performing for the fans rather than for their own enjoyment. In this view, athletes became degraded by taking money for their participation. A president of the IOC clearly articulated this sentiment many years later when he said "Sport must be amateur or it is not sport. Sports played professionally are entertainment."[2]

Students from England's Oxford University compete in rowing competitions. In the past, English rowing clubs restricted participation to amateurs in an effort to keep members of the lower classes from partaking in the sport.

The emphasis on amateurism had a side effect. To a large extent, restricting the Olympics to amateur athletes meant restricting the Games to the upper classes. If athletes were not permitted to make a living from sports, either they would have to work full time at a nonsports job—or they would have to be independently wealthy. People who have jobs have much less time for training and competition. As a result, most early Olympians were the sons of wealthy families. (Women competed in the Olympics for the first time in 1900.)

Indeed, the rules against professionals were designed partly to keep the "lower classes" out of the Olympics. Although Coubertin was French, his zeal for amateurism was heavily influenced by English sportsmen. The English definition of "amateur" went beyond not taking money for performances. Instead, it was based on social class. Most English rowing clubs, for example, barred all men who did manual labor, no matter how well they could row. On many occasions English rowers simply refused to race against foreign competition that included tradesmen.

Coubertin did not adopt the narrow English definition of amateur athletics for the 1896 Games. Salesmen, tradesmen, and others were permitted as long as they had never taken money for their athletic performances. Nevertheless, most competitors were amateurs, according even to the English model. This led to a controversy in the cycling road race. An Englishman named Edward Battel, a servant at the British embassy in Athens, entered the competition. Several other Englishmen, however, tried to keep Battel from competing. "He was not a gentleman," writes a historian, "and therefore was not in their eyes an amateur."[3] In the end, Battel was allowed to race; he finished third.

Coubertin was well aware of the class inequities created by the rule on amateurism. His solution was that wealthy men should come forward and sponsor deserving poor athletes. Rather than being paid to compete by race promoters and sports team owners, the patrons would give these athletes money to live on while continuing to train. However, Coubertin apparently never pushed hard for this

Avery Brundage, who competed in the Olympic Games and later served as the president of the IOC, ardently supported the decision to ban professionals from the Games.

solution; the original Olympic organizers never seriously considered it.

Ancient amateurs

In part, the founders of the Olympics based their disdain for professionals on the attitudes of the ancient Greeks. Coubertin and his friends believed that the early Olympians were all amateurs and were required to be so by Olympic rules. "The amateur code," said Avery Brundage, who competed with Thorpe in the 1912 decathlon and went on to serve for many years as IOC president, "coming to us from antiquity, embraces the highest moral laws. No philosophy, no religion, preaches loftier sentiments."[4] If amateurism was good enough for the ancients, the argument ran, it was worth putting in place for the modern Games as well.

However, recent scholarship has pretty well demolished the myth of ancient Greek amateurism. The ancient Olympians, even at the beginning, were true professionals. Some were given pensions after their careers were over. Others were supported in their training before their victories. It is not clear whether the early organizers were aware of the historical truth when they required amateurism for Olympians. But given the focus on amateur athletics in Britain and elsewhere, it is possible that knowing the truth about the ancient Greeks would not have made a difference.

Amateurism soon became established in the Olympic Code. As Jim Thorpe found out, taking any money at all could cost a competitor his medals. Finnish distance runner Paavo Nurmi, one of the most successful track stars in history, was banned from the 1932 Games just a week before the marathon. His offense was having accepted cash from a race promoter in excess of expenses. Even the value of gifts was strictly monitored. In 1947 Canadian Barbara Ann Scott won the figure skating world championships. She was given a new convertible by the people of her hometown. The IOC, however, told her that accepting the gift would make her a professional and therefore make her ineligible for the Winter Games of 1948. Scott gave the car back, competed in the Games, and won first place. When she turned professional later that year, the car was waiting for her.

Even teachers and coaches often ran afoul of the amateurism guidelines. According to Rule 26, amateurs could not profit in any way from their sports abilities and still remain eligible for Olympic competition. Coaches, even physical education instructors, got their jobs by virtue of their understanding of athletics. That made them suspect to the IOC. Australian swimmer Frank Beaurepaire, for instance, taught physical education and lectured on swimming and lifesaving to earn a living. This paid employment caused him to miss the 1912 Olympics. Even more puzzling was the fate of American Jean Shiley, who won a gold medal in 1932 and then was deemed ineligible for future Olympics. Like Beaurepaire, Shiley had once worked as a swimming teacher. Her medal, however, had come in the high jump!

The Soviets

Still, through the Second World War most people accepted the ban on professionals. In many sports, two levels developed over time: an amateur level, on which young performers competed, and a professional level, for later. Olympic boxers could give up their amateur standing to fight for money, and some became rich indeed. So could figure skaters, soccer players, and others. Those whose sports did not have much chance for professional advancement often became coaches at the Olympic or college level. While the system was far from perfect, not many observers were willing to fight for changes.

Then, in 1952, the Soviet Union sent a team to the Olympics for the first time in forty years. It was clear from the beginning of those Games that the Soviet team was different from those of the North American and western European nations that made up the majority of entries. The amateur Americans, West Germans, and French were mostly young. Many were high school or college students with little experience in their sports. The Soviets, on the other hand, sent athletes who were already veterans of international competitions.

Questioning amateurism

When the Soviets began to win medal after medal, some westerners questioned whether the eastern European athletes were truly amateurs. Of course they were, the Soviets responded. Their competitors held jobs—as soldiers, for instance, or teachers or students. They were not paid for their athletic performances. Skeptics, however, pressed for details: To what regiment did this rower belong? How long has that twenty-nine-year-old been in college? What grade level and subject did the shot-putter teach? The Soviets pointed out repeatedly that their collectivist system did not permit anything other than amateurism. "No such thing as [a] professional in a People's State,"[5] one journalist quoted a Soviet official as saying. In truth, at the time the Soviet Union and its satellite countries had no professional sports leagues, as westerners understood the concept, and did not permit their athletes to play in those of other nations.

Still, the Soviets' answers did not satisfy most westerners. It seemed to stretch the rules, if not to break them, to call a man an army captain when his main—perhaps only—duties involved training for the long jump, or to hire a teacher who spent the academic year competing in international speed-skating events. The athletes appeared to be professional in all but name, and it was hard for many observers to see why the soldier captain of the Soviet ice hockey team, say, was permitted to play in the Olympics while Canadian teams could not use equally experienced National Hockey League stars.

Not surprisingly, the "amateur" eastern athletes *were* usually far superior to anyone the West had to offer. American swimmers, boxers, and track stars grew tired of staying amateur—and poor—and moved on to new pursuits or professional sports. That was not so in Czechoslovakia, East Germany, or the Soviet Union. The Communist bloc

Members of the 1952 Soviet Olympic team mount a picture of Joseph Stalin on their dormitory in Helsinki, Finland. During the Games, the winning streak of the Soviets refueled the debate between the merits of amateurism and professionalism.

soon dominated sports in which they had no real tradition, such as soccer. Western nations tired of being beaten in what they called unfair contests. Finally, to protest the professionalism of the Soviet and Czech teams, Canada and Sweden refused to send ice hockey teams to the 1976 Winter Games in Innsbruck, Austria.

Scholarships

In 1952 Avery Brundage was elected head of the IOC, a position he would hold for twenty years. Brundage had a virulent hatred for professionalism of all kinds, and he saw the Soviet system as professionalism in disguise. As a way of removing all athletes who were not true amateurs, Brundage defined three classes of competitors who were professionals in all but label. Two of the classes applied specifically to eastern bloc countries:

> 1. So-called state amateurs—men who are taken from their usual vocation and either placed in camps for indefinite periods or given unusual opportunities to improve their performances.

> 2. Military personnel who are relieved of their normal duties for the same purpose.[6]

In 1952 Avery Brundage attempted to redefine professionalism to include college students on athletic scholarships. As a result, most college football players, like these from Baylor University's 1961 team, would be ineligible to compete in the Olympics.

However, Brundage did not merely go after the eastern nations. In fact, examples of his third class of false amateurs were found only in the West, the United States in particular. This class consisted of college students on athletic scholarships. Even by the 1940s, athletic scholarships were common in the United States. Then as now, they gave a gifted athlete free tuition in exchange for participation on a college sports team. In Brundage's eyes, the students

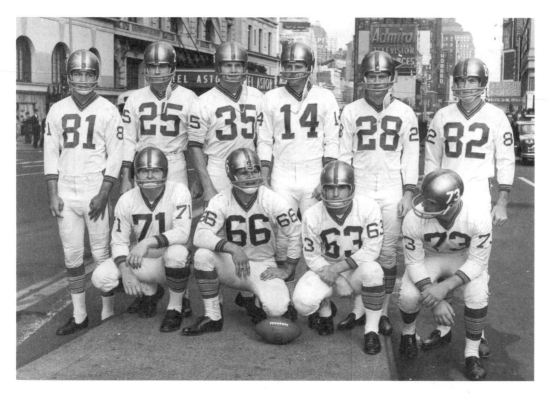

who accepted scholarships were professionals: they were receiving something of value solely for their athletic ability. "The gift of a scholarship worth several thousands of dollars," Brundage wrote, "is no different than a gift of several thousands of dollars in cash, and the truth is they are paid to participate."[7]

While many Americans disagreed with the contention that scholarships were the same as the practices of eastern bloc nations, others supported Brundage. "A southwestern football player who signs a contract with a university, receives thousands of dollars in academic aid and a fraudulent job from a prosperous alumnus is an amateur in America," said sportswriter Roger Kahn in 1964. "[Two-time bronze medalist] Igor Ter-Ovanesyan, [the Soviet Union's] best broad-jumper, has been attending a Moscow physical-fitness institute on what sounds like one of the best athletic scholarships in history, as good as anything a Big Ten quarterback gets."[8] Kahn's point was clear: the state support of the Russian athlete was essentially the same as the college's support of its star running back.

Backlash

Brundage's battles were doomed to failure, however. As competition became more intense during the 1950s and 1960s, it became increasingly hard to win an Olympic medal without devoting most of every day to training. The days when a gifted athlete could win the hammer throw or the high jump after only a few days of practice had vanished. Serious Olympic competitors needed money, whether through scholarships, government support, or pay from some other source. The alternatives were to take cash and lie about it, to starve, or to compromise training by holding down a full-time job. "If we followed Mr. Brundage's recommendations to their true end," one competitor warned, "then the Olympics would be a competition only for the very rich. No man of ordinary means could ever afford to excel in his sport."[9]

In fact, people outside the IOC increasingly saw the need for reform. Some said there was no significant difference between the professional and the amateur. "The champion so-called professional," wrote a 1964 observer,

> has exactly the same vision as the champion so-called amateur, and that is what chiefly motivates him. The differences in income, security, fame, etc., are strictly secondary. Both give the last full measure of devotion, from an instinct which is incomprehensible to the rest of us.[10]

Roger Kahn, writing in the same year, agreed.

> Have you ever seen Bill Russell leap to clear a backboard? Russell, the best basketball player in the world, is kept out of the Olympic basketball tournament because Olympic tradition argues that any athlete using his gifts to feed his children is impure.[11]

Still, the rules changed very slowly. In 1974, two years after Brundage retired, Rule 26 was amended to allow competitors to accept money to pay certain expenses, including coaching, some medical bills, and food and housing during training periods. Over the following years more changes were made. By the 1980s, most athletes were allowed to receive money from prizes, endorsements, and other sports-related sources. However, there was a catch: the money could not go directly to them; rather, it had to be deposited in a trust fund set up by their sport's governing body. Withdrawals from the account were acceptable if the athlete really needed cash. Otherwise, however, the money could not be touched until the athlete had officially retired from competition.

These changes were not approved by everyone. New questions arose. Some wondered who would decide how much cash could be withdrawn from an athlete's trust. Other observers disliked the inequities in the system. Athletes such as track star Carl Lewis lived very well—far better than less successful but equally "amateur" athletes in other sports. "The question many U.S. athletes in such non-glamour sports as fencing, rowing, or the discus ask themselves is not how much can I squeeze from an endorsement but how am I going to pay this month's rent?"[12] pointed out a 1988 magazine article. If the ideal was all athletes competing on an equal basis, then pay of any kind—even trust fund withdrawals—interfered with that goal.

Nevertheless, the trend continued. In 1987 the IOC allowed each sport to set its own eligibility requirements. Several sports, such as tennis, immediately dropped any amateur requirement, and many more, such as soccer, gymnastics, and ice hockey, began to move in that direction. Some observers have bemoaned the loss of the amateur ideal. As the *Toledo Blade* editorialized in 1989, after the Olympics were opened to truly professional basketball players, "Sure, Michael Jordan and others of his ilk no doubt would clear the boards and insure an American victory in basketball competition. . . . But is that what the Olympics should be about?"[13] After members of the 1998 U.S. hockey team vandalized a dormitory in the Olympic Village, one fan fired off a comment to an Internet bulletin board: "Bring the amateurs back to the [O]lympic [G]ames! Now! . . . We now get to see spoiled overpaid men instead of hard working energetic starry eyed kids at the [G]ames."[14]

Although changes in the IOC's regulations have benefited athletes in high-profile sports such as basketball and track and field, athletes competing in less popular sports, including fencing, have difficulty obtaining endorsements and making ends meet.

Some observers and athletes believe that Olympic sports have grown to be like professional sport leagues, and that in the process they have lost something. "With the pros swooping into the Olympics every 4 years to scoop up the medals, what incentive is there for a company or country to sponsor aspiring and largely anonymous 20-year-olds?"[15] a magazine asked in 1996. The question was about cycling, but it could be applied to almost any sport. "We're not in this sport because we like it or because we want to earn our way through school," American sprinter Leroy Burrell said in 1990. "We're in it to make money."[16] Many people shudder at statements like this.

Yet, in the opinion of some fans, the move to professionalism is all to the good. Certainly it serves to eliminate hypocrisy. "Amateurism in international athletics," editorialized a Connecticut paper, "is an appealing idea, but it's been a long time since Olympic athletes consisted solely of people who competed for personal or national triumph and nothing more. . . . The time has come to abandon the pretense."[17]

Allowing professionals into the Games, some observers believe, has also opened the doors to the finest athletes in the world. Under the new rules, a track coach points out, "mature people now, beyond the teeny-bopper stage, can make a dignified living at what they do best—run, jump, and throw."[18] The 1992 Olympics, said one writer, included "the greatest basketball team ever assembled"[19] in the persons of the largely professional U.S. "Dream Team" players. "The Olympic Games are a celebration of human excellence," said American IOC representative Anita DeFrantz in 1988, when the official move toward professionals was just starting. "Therefore the finest athletes should be eligible to compete."[20]

"Their hearts are pure"

As of late 1998, the governing body of nearly every Olympic sport had decided to allow professionals to compete in the Olympics. Among the few that continue to keep them out are baseball—although there is a movement to create teams of top professional players for 2004 and beyond—and boxing. Soccer also limits the age of professionals who compete in the Olympics. A few federations, notably figure skating, have complex rules about who is and who is not eligible; while technically these rules are based on professional and amateur status, the distinction has more to do with battles between various skating organizations than with money earned. Still, the system has changed. Amateurism, as Brundage and Coubertin saw it, has been eliminated.

Or has it? According to at least one writer, the current state of the Olympics expresses perhaps better than any the ideals of Coubertin. "On the one hand," said reporter Roger Angell about the 1996 U.S. men's basketball team made up of extremely wealthy NBA stars, "its members are the supreme symbol of the professionalization . . . of the Games. On the other hand, because the Games cannot offer enough gold . . . to turn their heads, their hearts are pure."[21] These professionals, in Angell's view, were competing only for joy and for the glory of their sport. No money or promises of personal fame would corrupt them.

The debate over amateurism is nearly over, and those who wanted the inclusion of professionals have certainly been the victors. It seems highly unlikely that the Olympics will ever again be restricted to amateurs. Within a few years even the few federations that still bar or restrict professionals may have relaxed their rules. The argument has been a long and costly one, however. There have been harsh words and wounded feelings on both sides. Most observers would agree that the original rules against professionalism had been applied too rigidly. But whether the goals of the Olympics are better served by having as competitors the best available athletes is still very much an open question.

2

Politics in the Games

Late in 1979 the Soviet Union sent troops into its neighboring nation of Afghanistan. The invasion was decried by most of the western world. President Jimmy Carter denounced the invasion as a "callous violation of international law and the United Nations Charter,"[22] and the leaders of many other governments agreed with the U.S. position. Over a hundred nations signed a resolution condemning the Soviet invasion. Despite the international pressure, however, the Soviet government refused to pull its troops out of Afghanistan.

As world leaders cast around for a meaningful way to express their concerns, one possibility stood out. The 1980 Summer Olympic Games were to be held in Moscow, the capital of the Soviet Union. The Soviets were looking forward to hosting the Games and to the accompanying worldwide publicity. Several western leaders, led by President Carter, decided to use the Moscow Games to pressure the Soviets. In April 1980, the U.S. Olympic Committee (USOC) voted by a two-to-one margin not to send a team to Moscow as a way of registering protest. This boycott quickly gathered steam, principally among nations allied with the United States; in the end, more than sixty countries followed the USOC's lead.

The boycott

Reaction to the boycott varied considerably. Some athletes were especially upset. Most had spent years training for an opportunity to appear in the Games. For many, the

1980 Olympics would have been their only chance. "These are *our* Games," argued hurdler Edwin Moses. "Just what right does Carter have to keep us from going?"[23] Others—athletes and nonathletes alike—questioned whether the boycott would have any practical effect. British runner Sebastian Coe called it a "fruitless exercise" that could not help the Afghan people in any meaningful way.[24]

But the largest question in the minds of those who opposed the boycott was whether it was wise to allow the invasion to dictate participation in the Games. To keep a team home because of the political policies of the host nation struck some observers as the wrong choice. "My personal feeling is that politics and sports shouldn't be mixed,"[25] said the coach of the 1980 U.S. boxing team. Perhaps, some argued, there were better ways of expressing disapproval. A Danish official advocated sending teams but not taking part in the opening and closing ceremonies. Olympic historian David Wallechinsky suggests that American athletes might have "display[ed] Afghani flags during the Parade of Nations."[26]

Sports and politics

However, the boycott had plenty of support as well. Polls showed that a large majority of the American people applauded the action. Several athletes—among them New Zealand runner Dick Quax and U.S. pole vaulter Jeff Taylor—spoke out in favor of the boycott. "It seems crazy to me that . . . Russia's sending an army into Afghanistan doesn't seem to disturb some people,"[27] lamented Quax. Many western officials agreed. "There is something repellent about Soviet troops being in Afghanistan at the same time . . . doves are being let loose in Moscow,"[28] said a U.S. State Department official. As for the notion that politics should never be mixed with sport, many leaders argued that such a viewpoint was simply naive. "In an ideal world," said British prime minister Margaret Thatcher, "I would share entirely the philosophy of the international Olympic movement that sport should be divorced from politics. Sadly, however, this is no longer a realistic view."[29]

Whether boycotting the 1980 Olympics was proper is still debated. Hindsight does not settle the question. But the 1980 experience is by no means unique in Olympic history. Politics have been an issue since the beginning of the Games. The annals of the Olympics are filled with boycotts, near-boycotts, expulsions of countries, and biased judging. Athletes, governments, and outsiders alike have attempted to use the Games for political ends. Often, politics and nationalism have served as weapons to settle petty disagreements between countries or as wedges to drive nations further apart.

Coubertin and politics

The original conception of the modern Olympics had little place for nationalism of any kind. Coubertin's idea, in fact, was that the Olympics would be so free from political influence that the Games would actually help promote peace. As he wrote,

> Wars break out because nations misunderstand each other. We shall not have peace until the prejudices which now separate the different races shall have been outlived. To attain this end, what better means than to bring the youth of all countries periodically together for amicable trials of muscular strength and agility?[30]

The Games were designed to play up the similarities between nations, not the differences. Coubertin's image of a group of international sportsmen paving the way toward world peace was a strong one in the late nineteenth century. Indeed, it was a major factor in persuading so many other countries to join France in the Olympic movement.

Once again, Coubertin got some of his ideas from the ancient Olympics. In this case, however, his history was mostly accurate. The ancient Olympics did serve a peaceful purpose. While fighting continued elsewhere in the Greek world, the so-called Olympic truce covered athletes and spectators on their way to and from the Games. Thus the period covered by the Games were perhaps the safest time for Greek travelers in general.

There is also evidence, however, that the ancient peoples cared very much about results involving athletes from their particular region. "Many [regions], and especially those in south Italy and Sicily, made strenuous efforts to obtain athletic victors," writes a historian of the Games. "They recruited athletes and trainers . . . built luxurious training facilities, bribed judges, sacrificed lavishly, and prayed."[31] A victory for an athlete was a victory for the people he represented as well.

Coubertin was aware of this, too, and he agreed that nationalism could be a positive force in making the modern Olympics more exciting. "One may be filled with a desire to see the color of one's club or college triumph in a national meeting," he wrote; "but how much stronger is the feeling when the colors of one's country are at stake!"[32] However, Coubertin also saw nationalism as a possible danger. Excessive nationalism, he believed, could ultimately corrupt or even destroy the Games.

Thus, Coubertin tried to play down nationalist elements while still allowing people to cheer for their own athletes. The winners of the various events had the flags of their countries raised at the victory celebrations, for example; but all athletes competed only as individuals, not as members of teams. Indeed, the 1896 Games included no team sports of any kind: no swimming or track relays, and no combined-scores competition in sports such as gymnastics.

The 1980 gold medal–winning U.S. hockey team (in the background) takes part in the medals presentation ceremony. Although the United States hosted the 1980 Winter Games at Lake Placid, New York, U.S. teams boycotted the Summer Games in Moscow for political reasons.

Coubertin specifically discouraged nations from keeping track of their successes and failures at the Games. Rule 9 of the Olympic Charter puts it quite clearly: "The Games are contests between individuals and not between countries."[33]

Coubertin's ideas have been better followed during some Games than others. The flag raising, coupled now with the playing of national anthems, still exists, and athletes continue to be identified by country. Most of the time—though not always—fans cheer for each competitor. On the other hand, team sports, which are more obviously nationalist in character, have slowly crept in. The recent trend has been toward more and more emphasis on team sports such as basketball, softball, and ice hockey, and the team aspects of individual sports like gymnastics and track.

Standings

Coubertin was displeased when countries bragged about their athletes' Olympic victories, but his disapproval has not kept nations from doing exactly that. Nearly all unofficial histories of the Games, along with most media coverage of the Games as they are happening, present readers with extensive tables showing the number of medals won by each country. Along with the flags and anthems, this scorekeeping is probably the most obvious example of nationalism in the Olympics.

Most observers agree that keeping score and waving flags are relatively harmless. Tracking medal winnings can create a friendly rivalry between countries. Nations suffering from internal strife can sometimes come together over an especially memorable performance, and the deeds of a team or an individual can inspire a healthy national pride. Nor does a team need to post a spectacular success to have this effect. "For newly independent people like the Latvians," wrote a reporter during the 1994 Winter Olympics, "just seeing television images of the national team carrying the country's flag in an Olympic parade feels as good as winning the gold."[34]

Moreover, keeping charts can be entertaining. "Winning a race does not prove one nation 'better' than another," a journalist admitted in a 1956 article; "probably winning a war doesn't prove it, either. Yet the results are simply too interesting, chastening, inspiring, to be ignored."[35] To a degree, medal standings pique interest in the Olympics. "Nationalism seems an attraction, not an impediment, to the Games,"[36] concluded a journalist a generation later. The occasional calls for "stateless" Olympics, without flags and anthems, strike most observers as misguided.

However, flags and scoreboards can be carried too far. There was much hand-wringing during the 1950s over the Olympic rivalry between the Soviet Union and the United States. The two countries were political enemies to begin with, and the Olympic competitions only made things worse. The Soviet Union and the United States each devised an informal scoring system to try to "prove" that its athletes were better. During the 1956 Games, the IOC issued a reminder that "there is no official score by nations, and tables of points are entirely inaccurate."[37] This well-meaning bulletin was notably unsuccessful. "One day later," observed a reporter, "headlines all over the world clarioned the news that Russia had taken a 43-35 lead over the United States."[38]

The U.S. and Soviet basketball teams square off during the 1972 Olympics. For decades both countries shared a vicious rivalry, bringing the cold war to the fields of competition.

Judging

In Coubertin's words, "the important thing in the Olympic Games is not winning but taking part."[39] In an ideal world, the Olympics would stay free of political pressures for one competitor or team to win. In practice, however, the Games have been full of questionable decisions, clearly demonstrating that—in the eyes of some judges and administrators, in any case—winning is more important than anything else.

An early example of this came in the Lake Placid Winter Games of 1932. The first Winter Olympics, held in France in 1924, had used a two-competitor format for speed-skating events. Two athletes skated together around a track; after all competitors had skated, the one with the fastest time was declared the winner. Upon arriving for the speed-skating competitions, Europeans were told that the races would be held using a very different format: all skaters would leave the start at once, and the first to cross the finish line would

South Korean boxer Park Si-hun lifts American Roy Jones off the canvas after their hotly debated match during the 1988 Olympics. Although judges awarded Si-hun the gold medal, the boxer did not feel he had won the bout.

be the winner. The U.S. men's team, which already knew about the change, went on to win all four available gold medals, giving them precisely half the total won by U.S. male speed skaters through 1972.

Judges, too, have voted along political lines in judged sports. In one notable case, South Korean boxer Park Si-hun won five extremely controversial matches on his way to a 1988 gold medal in his home country. The final victory surprised even him. "I am sorry," he told the silver medalist. "I lost the fight."[40] Judges in figure skating and gymnastics routinely give out higher scores to competitors from their own nations. In a 1998 figure skating pairs competition, for instance, the American judge rated an American couple first after the short program. Only one other judge rated them as high as third. The Mexican winner of a men's 1956 diving contest was particularly upset by biased judging. "It amounted to a competition between the nationalities of the judges rather than a competition of divers,"[41] he complained afterward.

Once in a while, nationalistic passions burst out between the athletes themselves. The Soviet-Hungary water polo match of 1956 was a particularly dramatic example. Hungary had just been invaded by the Soviets, and anger among the Hungarians ran high. The pool was soon tinged with blood, as players seemingly became more interested in injuring their opponents than in scoring goals. As one writer pointed out, "one was not witnessing nationalism [in the match] but war."[42]

Fans and the media, too, can take nationalism too seriously, thus diverting attention from an athlete's accomplishments. "She may win a gold medal for the U.S.,"[43] read the subhead of a 1984 article about gymnast Mary Lou Retton. Retton did win a gold medal, but of course the medal represented an individual accomplishment; it was not an award for the entire country. "The honor of the flag is *not* involved," cautioned a 1955 article lamenting the lack of sportsmanship among U.S. Olympic fans and reporters, "when a foreign contestant finishes a tenth of a second ahead of an American in the 100-meter dash."[44]

Political rivalries can sometimes lead to bloody altercations when opposing teams vie for superiority in the Olympic arena. Here, an injured member of the 1956 Hungarian water polo team seeks medical attention after participating in a violent match with the Soviets.

Cancellations and expulsions

For the most part, the intrusions of politics have been small and have not seriously disrupted the Olympics. Sometimes, however, politics have entered the Games on a much larger scale. Three times since 1896 the Games have been canceled altogether because the world was at war. The Olympics of 1916, 1940, and 1944 were games that never were. "In ancient days," mourned Avery Brundage, though not quite accurately, "nations stopped wars to compete in the Games. Nowadays we stop the Olympics to continue our wars."[45] Even Brundage had to admit, however, that it would have been hard to hold the 1944 Games in London, according to the schedule set years earlier, since the city was under constant attack.

Beyond those three cancellations, however, politics have helped to determine which countries participate and which do not. In a few cases, nations have been barred from competing by the rest of the IOC. One of the earliest bans affected Germany, generally considered the aggressor in Europe in World Wars I and II. As punishment, Germany was barred from competing in the Games of 1920, 1924, and 1948. (The Japanese were also banned from competition in 1948.) A later ban affected South Africa, which had a political system called apartheid, in which the black majority of its citizens was denied rights enjoyed by the

American gymnast Mary Lou Retton won a gold medal for her performance in the 1984 Olympic Games. Although Retton won the medal by her participation on the U.S. team, critics argue that such accomplishments are personal rather than national ones.

South African runner Zola Budd competes in the 1984 Olympics. Since her home country of South Africa was banned from competing in the Games, Budd had to qualify as a British citizen in order to participate.

white minority. This ban lasted until 1992, when apartheid was abolished and a black majority government came to power. A handful of other nations have also been banned for a time, most notably the militarily aggressive Yugoslavia in 1992.

The expulsions have not been terribly controversial in themselves. Few IOC members stuck up for Yugoslavia's violations of human rights in 1992 or supported South African apartheid—at least, not publicly. Yet the banning of entire countries outright has raised a few questions. One is whether athletes should be treated as individuals or as citizens of their respective nations. In 1984 and again in 1988, the IOC ran into controversy when a white South African runner named Zola Budd attempted to compete. Some saw Budd as a symbol of apartheid and vehemently opposed her participation; at one international race, protesters held up signs that read "White Trash Go Home."[46] Others argued that Budd, while a South African, was first and foremost a runner, not a political symbol, and ought to be permitted to take part. "She did not invent that system," editorialized an Oregon newspaper, "she took no part in South African politics, and she never has been accused of acting like a racist."[47]

The IOC did not to relax its ban on South Africa, but Budd ultimately competed in 1984 by qualifying as a British citizen. A few years later, the IOC compromised in its treatment of Yugoslavia. While Yugoslavia could not compete as a nation and no flags or anthems would be allowed, the country's athletes could participate as individuals, calling themselves "Independent Olympic Participants."

Where should the IOC draw the line? Many nations with dismal records on human rights have not been banned from competition, as South Africa was. Many more have used terror and war as a weapon, again without being ejected from the Olympic movement. "There's no question about apartheid being a deplorable policy," said an Arizona newspaper during the Budd controversy. Nevertheless, the paper asked, "Why is apartheid deemed so much more reprehensible than, say, state terrorism? Where is the . . . indignation over the domestic policies of [Olympic competitors] Cuba, Syria, Libya, or North Korea?"[48] The IOC has left itself open to charges of hypocrisy when it has banned certain nations from competing while accepting as competitors citizens of countries vulnerable to criticism on the same or similar charges.

Boycotts

In 1936, several western democracies considered boycotting the Berlin Olympics to express their opposition to the Nazi government in Germany, just as many nations kept their teams home from Moscow in 1980, as a protest against Soviet expansionism. The 1936 boycott came to nothing, however. Concerns over mixing politics and sports, combined with poor organization among those in favor of staying home, helped doom the proposal.

Not all political boycotts have protested the policies of the host country. The first Olympic boycott, for example, occurred in 1956. In that year Spain and the Netherlands protested the Soviet invasion of Hungary by refusing to send teams to the Melbourne Games, while Egypt, Lebanon, and Iraq stayed home because forces from Britain and France had taken over the Suez Canal. Other boycotts have focused on the identity of certain competitors. For example, in 1976 African nations demanded the expulsion of New Zealand's athletes on the grounds that a rugby team from that country had played in South Africa, still banned because of apartheid. The IOC refused to ask the New Zealanders to leave, and accordingly many black-majority countries boycotted the Montreal Games.

Boycotts are a clear reminder that the Olympic Games are not above politics. "Now politics has entered into an event intended to be devoted exclusively to enthusiastic, competitive sports,"[49] mourned a reporter as the 1956 Games got under way. This reality can be very hard for Olympic athletes, fans, and officials alike to accept. The world is "fed up with politicians interfering with sport,"[50] said IOC president Lord Killanin in 1976.

A question of human rights

Part of the point of an Olympic boycott is to drive home the message that sports are not more important than human rights, security, or the ideal of world peace. Nations that participate in such boycotts generally believe that their complaint is so important that they are justified in drawing attention to it by disrupting the supposedly nonpolitical Olympics. Commonly, they are careful not to call the boycotts purely political. "When the Soviet Union crossed the borders of Afghanistan with a brutal invasion," Jimmy Carter wrote in explaining the 1980 boycott, "the basic principles of the Olympics were violated."[51] Similarly, Uganda rejected the notion that its boycott of the 1976 Games was just an attempt to apply "political pressure." Instead, Ugandan officials argued, they were waging "a fight against apartheid in sport."[52] Still, many boycotts do result from a notion that some principles are bigger than the Olympics.

Regardless of whether boycotts are justified, the people most affected by these actions have always been the athletes. Some have gone to great lengths to try to compete despite a walkout. In 1976 James Gilkes, a runner from the boycotting nation of Guyana, petitioned the IOC to allow him to participate under the Olympic flag, but the IOC turned him down. In 1980 judo competitor Yasuhiro Yamashita went on national television in Japan to plead with his national sports federation not to join the U.S.-led boycott. His plea was to no avail: Japan stayed home.

Boycotts have also deprived fans of some long-awaited matchups between individuals and teams. "It's too bad the

Cubans won't be there," mused an editorial about the 1988 Games in Seoul, South Korea, which Cuba and a handful of other nations decided not to attend. "Their boxers and baseball players are as good as any."[53] The boycott of the Los Angeles Games by most eastern bloc countries, in 1984, wrote a reporter, "deprives U.S. [swimming] stars Tracy Caulkins and Mary T. Meagher of a chance to prove once and for all that they're No. 1 in their events."[54] Consecutive boycotts in 1980 by Americans and 1984 by Soviets meant that showdowns between athletes from these two athletic powerhouses did not occur between 1976 and 1988.

More protests

The Games have also seen examples of political protest by athletes—miniboycotts, in a sense. In the early 1900s, for instance, Finland was governed by Russia, and its athletes competed for the Russian team. Some Finnish athletes, however, caused a stir when they refused to march behind the Russian flag in the opening ceremonies. The 1936 marathon champion, Sohn Kee-chung, was a Korean forced by Japan to compete as a Japanese; some record books still list him under his Japanese name of Kitei Son. During the medal ceremony, Sohn bowed his head rather than acknowledge the Japanese flag. Similarly, two American track winners at the 1968 Games bowed their heads and raised clenched fists as they stood on the victory platform in an expression of African-American solidarity. (The IOC found the gesture inappropriate: it suspended the Americans and ordered them to leave the Olympic Village at once.)

The politicization of the Games continues. One website urges a boycott of the 2000 Olympics in Sydney. Australia, according to the boycott's organizers, is "an outlaw nation whose racial policies are little different from apartheid South Africa."[55] Several Islamic nations with conservative religious governments refuse to send female competitors to the Games; this has caused some European and African feminists to call for an Olympic boycott until the IOC forces those countries to include women. As long as the

Olympics continue, people are likely to want to use them for political ends.

An international showcase

In fact, the very success of the Games encourages their use as a political tool. With the eyes of the world on the Games, boycotts and expulsions become a cheap and easy way for nations to gain publicity for their political agendas. Sadly, some of the methods have been violent. At the Munich Games in 1972, a group of terrorists made their way into the Olympic Village and murdered eleven Israeli athletes and coaches. Sportscaster Jim McKay called it "the worst day in the history of sport."[56] The

U.S. Olympians Tommie Smith (center) and John Carlos (right) raise clenched fists and bow their heads during the 1968 medal ceremony. The track stars were protesting the treatment of blacks in the United States.

Games have been threatened by terrorists at other times as well. The 1992 Barcelona Olympics needed extra security because of threats made by separatist groups in Spain; fortunately, there were no incidents. During the 1988 Seoul Games there were also heightened tensions owing to the hostility between North and South Korea. Again, the events were peaceful.

Yet, despite the intrusion of politics, it is important to remember what the Games *have* accomplished. The majority of Olympiads have done just what Coubertin wanted: they have brought athletes of many nations together in an atmosphere of peace and appreciation. Perhaps the wonder is not that political turmoil has gotten in the way of the Games, but that the Games have survived so well despite unsettled times and national enmities. As one newspaper put it, "The Games themselves . . . stand as a symbol of cooperative competition among peoples of this planet. . . . We should all look forward to the day that the Olympics will stand for these things alone, and politics will be left at home."[57]

Indeed, in many ways politics already is left at home. The Olympics are very often a truly nonpolitical affair. It is quite common for a national hero to become an international one. The whole world has applauded the athletic feats of stars such as Norwegian speed skater Johan Olav Koss, Romanian gymnast Nadia Comaneci, and American track star Jackie Joyner-Kersee. When U.S. skater Dan Jansen won a gold medal in 1994 after years of disappointment, the Official Report of the Games concluded, "At that moment there were no Norwegians, Dutch, Americans or people of other nationalities among the spectators, only fans of Dan Jansen."[58]

Moreover, few other events bring countries together as the Olympics have. Nations that refuse to acknowledge each other diplomatically have met at the Olympics. Nations whose political and economic systems were violently opposed have come together at the Games, and in some cases their athletes have become friends. At the height of the cold war, American Olympian Dick Hamilton discovered that the Russian competitors were not the

American speed skater Dan Jansen sets a new world record while competing in the 1,000-meter race at the 1994 Olympics. When Jansen finally won the gold medal after years of competition, it was an emotional moment shared by the world.

"arrogant, hardened group of athletes" he had believed them to be, but a team made up of men who, as he put it, "make a point of shaking the hand of the American who [has] just beaten him."[59]

In 1992, when South Africa at last was readmitted to the Olympics, a black Ethiopian and a white South African finished first and second in a distance race. Following the race, the two took a victory lap together, a lap that one writer said "seemed to symbolize hope for a new Africa."[60] Perhaps the greatest success of the Olympics over the years lies in moments such as these—moments that transcend the political squabbles of the world and indeed "symbolize hope" for something better.

3

Commercialism

OF ALL THE controversies in Olympic history, certainly one of the most bizarre occurred in 1992 at Barcelona, Spain. The U.S. basketball "Dream Team," made up mainly of seasoned professionals, dominated the men's tournament, as they had been expected to do. The gold medal game had just ended and the medal ceremony was about to begin when the controversy arose. There had been no allegations of cheating during the games, nor had there been any question of the pros' status as legitimate competitors; the issue had nothing to do with politics or with discrimination of any kind. Instead, the controversy swirled around—uniforms.

Before the 1992 Games began, the U.S. Olympic Committee had raised money by selling sponsorships to various corporations. Among the companies that rushed to support the team was the shoe manufacturer Reebok, which bought the right to sponsor the uniforms that would be worn by all U.S. medal winners. Reebok gave the USOC a payment that covered the cost of making the outfits and much more besides. In return, the USOC granted Reebok certain major concessions: the company was allowed both to call itself an official sponsor of the Games in its advertising and to use the victory uniforms themselves to advertise its shoes. Reebok did exactly that, placing a Reebok logo on every uniform it produced for the USOC.

For most athletes, the Reebok logo did not present a problem. But several of the American basketball players, including the Chicago Bulls' Michael Jordan, were already under personal contracts to Nike, one of Reebok's fiercest competitors. They rejected the idea of putting on a uniform with a Reebok logo—even a small, unobtrusive logo for a five-minute ceremony—and refused to go onto the victory stand in the Reebok outfits.

The U.S. Olympic Committee gathered quickly and before long had hammered out a compromise. In the end, the whole team made it onto the podium in time for the playing of the U.S. national anthem. All were wearing the standard uniforms with the Reebok insignia. The players under contract with Nike, however, had hidden the logo under strips of tape and American flag pins to avoid any appearance of a conflict of interest.

The Nike-Reebok controversy plays up an important issue in the recent history of the Olympics: the role of corporate funding. The money paid to the Olympics by large businesses has helped the Olympics grow, and perhaps even to survive. Yet that money comes with strings attached.

The power wielded by the corporations that give the money is growing all the time, and not always in ways healthy or helpful to the goals of the Olympic movement.

Early restrictions

The commercialization of the Games is fairly recent. The 1896 Olympics had no corporate sponsors. The Games were simply not important enough to matter to the business community. Only thirteen nations took part, and there was no guarantee that the competition would ever be repeated. Moreover, advertising was still in its infancy in 1896. The concept of linking a product with a feel-good event such as the Olympics—and paying for the privilege—was not yet widespread, and the idea of an athlete endorsing a product was likewise rare.

The most important reason for the lack of commercialism, though, may have been Coubertin's vision of sport as pure and uncorrupted. Just as Coubertin worried that money might corrupt the athletes by changing their focus, he feared that corporate involvement could corrupt the Games by emphasizing the ideal of money—rather than the ideals of fair play and doing one's best.

The 1896 Olympics, however, were not the only ones to avoid commercial links. Even as the advertising age grew and the Olympics became more visible to a worldwide audience, the IOC stood firm against any sign of corporate influence. Rule 58 of the Olympic charter, which was in effect as late as the 1970s, said it quite clearly:

> No [commercial] publicity whatsoever shall be allowed in the sky above the stadia and other Olympic areas. . . . Advertising signs shall not be permitted inside the stadium or other sports arenas. No advertising is permitted on equipment used in the Olympic Games nor on the uniforms or numbers worn by contestants.[61]

Rule 58 went on to ban nearly all kinds of advertising contract between the Games and corporations. The rule also restricted advertising on clothes worn in the Olympic Village. Even the trademarks on timing equipment and scoreboards were regulated: under no circumstances could these logos be more than ten centimeters high, and that only in the case of a large surface.

Well before the 1970s, however, Rule 58 was being broken. A handful of athletes ran afoul of the no-advertising rules as early as the 1930s. The great all-around athlete Mildred "Babe" Didrikson Zaharias, for instance, was banned from the Games forever for letting a car company use her name in its advertising. Learning from Zaharias's example, other athletes were somewhat more cautious. Bans on competitors for violating Rule 58 were few. Still, there is little doubt that some companies did make regular payments to athletes as early as the 1950s, perhaps even before. IOC chief Avery Brundage made it his special mission to smoke these competitors out, but he had great difficulty finding proof.

Thirties great Mildred "Babe" Didrikson Zaharias was among the first athletes to be forever banned from competing in the Olympic Games for breaking the IOC's Rule 58, which banned athletes from participating in corporate advertising.

Brundage vs. Schranz

While payments to athletes were known in swimming, in track, and in most other Olympic sports, they were most prevalent in the Winter Games, and most notably in alpine skiing. The reason was simple: money was essential to a world-class competitive skier. Ski racers needed carefully groomed trails to practice on; that meant paying to use the trails owned by ski resorts. Qualifying races were held all over the world, so travel costs were high, sometimes exorbitant. Most of all, skis were expensive. So were boots, gloves, and poles. There was no point in trying to compete with less than the best equipment. Thus, even well-off skiers often were in need of money to continue their training. The easiest sources of money were the corporations that manufactured the gear skiers needed to win. The richest ski makers hurried to sign the top athletes to secret contracts, promising them free equipment and extra cash if the skiers would use their products and make them as visible as possible.

As time went on, the corporate money in alpine skiing grew. In the early 1960s, Brundage claimed that thirty to forty of the best skiers were in the pay of ski companies.

Some were on company payrolls as "ski testers" or the like, while others were given cash as needed. "When a skier insists on being photographed showing the brand of his skis we can be sure there is a reason," Brundage said in 1968, "even if we cannot prove it."[62] His implication was clear. That skier was accepting payments from a corporation—an act in direct defiance of Rule 58. Upset at what he saw as outrageous flouting of the rules, Brundage wrote a bylaw in 1968 that required Olympic ski medalists to give their skis to police officers before being photographed.

In 1972 Brundage went further. Just before the Sapporo Olympics that year, he persuaded the IOC to ban Austrian star skier Karl Schranz from competing. Schranz, like most other top skiers, was rumored to be earning close to $50,000 a year from ski manufacturers. Unlike most other top skiers, however, Schranz had been especially outspoken in his criticism of Brundage and his policies. Schranz went, but not quietly. "If Mr. Brundage had been poor, as I was, and as were many other athletes," he said, "I wonder if he wouldn't have a different attitude."[63] Other athletes came to his defense, and Austrian ski fans began calling Brundage "the senile millionaire from Chicago."[64] Schranz never competed again, but like Jim Thorpe, he was eventually rehabilitated. In 1988 the IOC awarded him a symbolic medal as a participant in the 1972 Games.

Austrian skier Karl Schranz was banned from competing in the 1972 Olympics on suspicions that he was subsidized by ski manufacturers and had thus violated Rule 58.

Montreal, 1976

While athletes have been taking corporate money, legally or not, for years, the same has not been true of the Games themselves. Corporate sponsorship of the Olympics was slow to catch on. For many years it was uncommon for Olympic committees to accept cash even if approached by a company: Rule 58, while hard to monitor where individual athletes were concerned, was much less difficult to enforce in the case of entire organizations.

During the 1970s, however, this situation began to change. The first reason for the change was television, a force unknown in the early days of the century. Television's power grew slowly: not until 1960 did Olympic competitions become a staple of American television. But as technology improved and interest in televised sports grew, the television industry became a major player at the Olympics. In 1972 ABC paid the IOC $13 million to broadcast the Munich Games on American TV. For ABC, the investment was well worth it. Advertisers jumped at the chance to peddle their products on national television, and they were not disappointed: Americans were a large portion of the estimated one *billion* people worldwide who watched part of the Games that year.

But the advertisers and the ABC network were not alone in making money. The IOC benefited handsomely as well. By the late 1960s, the IOC had developed a system for distributing the revenue from television contracts. One-third of the take went to the IOC itself, which distributed most of it to the Olympic Committees of various nations. The other two-thirds was to go to the host city to help defray costs. Even as early as the 1972 Olympics, it was clear that the television revenues could allow organizers to spend money they otherwise would not have had. Because the television money ultimately came from advertisers, the advertisers found themselves thrust into the role of supporting the Olympics. Despite restrictions on ads on stadium signs, uniforms, and scoreboards, the Games were nevertheless beholden to corporations and their advertising money.

Another nudge toward commercialism came when three consecutive Summer Games—Mexico City in 1968, Munich in 1972, and Montreal in 1976—suffered financial losses. The 1976 experience was particularly stark. While the Montreal Games were designed to be expensive, costs soon spiraled out of control. Officials scaled plans further and further back—a proposed television tower was scrapped, the roof of the Olympic Stadium was left off—and yet the organizers dropped deeper into debt. In the end the 1976 Games cost what observers considered a "scandalous"[65]

Throngs of spectators and athletes assemble in Montreal's Olympic Stadium to witness the opening ceremonies of the 1976 Olympic Games. After spending hundreds of millions of dollars to host the international competition, organizers of the Montreal Games were faced with an enormous deficit.

amount. Estimates range into the hundreds of millions of dollars, much of it coming from Canadian taxpayers.

In retrospect, it is clear that the Montreal experience was unusual. Organizers that year faced problems that have affected no other Olympics before or since. But in 1976, that truth was far from evident. When the world looked at the Olympics, it saw three debt-ridden Games in a row, with the problem apparently growing worse. Just a few years after the Montreal Games, writer Leonard Koppett stated that "it has become prohibitively expensive" to build new sites for an Olympic Games.[66] In his estimation, all future Olympics either would bankrupt their hosts or would be held in cities that already had the necessary stadiums, housing, and transportation systems: that is, cities that had held the Games before. Indeed, there were few bidders for the 1980 Games eventually hosted by Moscow, and only one serious contender for 1984.

The Los Angeles proposal

While the Montreal Games were losing money, however, a handful of sources did manage to provide some income. Lotteries were run across Canada, with proceeds to go to the deficit. Commemorative stamps and coins were sold as well, a tactic pioneered in Munich four years earlier. The income showed that Olympic fans were interested in paying for Olympic memorabilia. Television rights fees continued to climb, which helped, too. And another $6 million came from selling advertising rights to the mascot of the Games, Amik the beaver, concession rights to making and marketing official Olympic posters, and the commercial use of the logo of the 1976 Games.

Six million dollars was very little compared to the deficit, but the acquisition of money through licensing, advertising, and corporate sponsorships was widely noted. In 1978 Los Angeles presented a bid to the IOC for the 1984 Games, a bid that called for as much corporate support of the Games as possible. Instead of saddling taxpayers with the bill or relying on wealthy individuals to pay expenses, the Los Angeles Olympics would be funded primarily by corporate sponsorships. Moreover, the Los Angeles Committee said that it would keep all the television money for itself, instead of sharing a third of it with the IOC. This money, organizers said, would be used to help defray any unexpected costs.

Swimmers dive into a pool during the 1984 Olympics in Los Angeles. The city's bid to host the Games, which was the only one submitted to the IOC, called for an increase in corporate sponsorship in order to offset the incredible expenses.

The Los Angeles bid took IOC members by surprise. Many were uncomfortable with the blatant commercialism of the idea. Others were furious at what they considered to be the city's high-handedness in claiming all the television revenues. A reporter talked to a dozen IOC members after the bid had been distributed; "most of them," he remembered, "favored rejecting the bid out of hand and without further discussion."[67] In the end, though, they did not. Part of the reason was that Los Angeles was the only applicant for the Games. Moreover, after much discussion it became evident to most committee members that a change in the system was necessary. The alternative was, as Koppett had predicted, that the ranks of prospective hosts for future Olympics would shrink to a handful of cities.

"Proud to be the official outfitter"

Once Los Angeles had the Olympics, committee members started auctioning off rights to the 1984 Games to the highest bidders. There was no shortage of corporations eager to associate themselves with the Games. "Levi Strauss & Co. is proud to be the official outfitter of the 1984 U.S. Olympic team,"[68] read one advertisement. Michelob advertisements showed a close-up of a beer glass emblazoned with the name of the company, the letters "USA," and the interlocking Olympic rings. McDonald's donated money to build the "McDonald's Olympic Swim Stadium"[69] for the Games. Purists decried the emphasis on commercialism. But when the Games were over, no one could argue with the financial picture. Aside from security costs, taxpayers were hardly affected. There was no Montreal-style deficit; indeed, there was no deficit. The organizing committee reported a profit of $215 million.

The Games of 1984 set a new trend. Every succeeding Olympics has seemingly had more sponsors and more commercial tie-ins than the one before. In all, corporations paid $400 million to be associated with the 1996 Atlanta Games. Advertising is, truly, everywhere: in the venues, on the competitors, on the airwaves. Ice hockey players in 1998 all wore uniforms with Nike swooshes. Athletes who went to Barcelona in 1992 lived in the Bausch & Lomb Olympic Village. NBC paid a stunning $456 million for the Atlanta Olympics—about 33 times what ABC had paid in 1972 and up from $401 million in Barcelona.

Just as the Games have benefited from corporate money, many athletes, too, have been helped by commercial sponsorship. Money from shoe companies, equipment makers, or soft drink firms has enabled runners, skiers, and swimmers alike to devote their full energies to sports. Swimmer Daniel Kowalski, who won three medals in 1996, is one of several young Australian Olympians known as "Team Ford," after the car company that underwrites their training. Slalom specialist Alberto Tomba received comparable assistance from the Rossignol ski company. Reebok sponsored decathletes Dan O'Brien and Dave Johnson, and Mizuno was one of many corporations that helped support track star Carl Lewis.

Less well-known competitors receive corporate money, too. Money from Kodak, IBM, and other Olympic sponsors goes to national Olympic committees, which then pass some of it on to athletes in the form of free room and board, free medical care, and free coaching. Some athletes are paid a stipend as well. Another portion of the money helps provide better coaching, better training facilities, and advances in technology and research which can lead to better equipment. The Arco Corporation, for instance, donated $15 million to help build a training center for U.S. Olympians in Chula Vista, California. Directly and indirectly, these payments go to help athletes focus on their training and improve their performance.

Murdering sportsmanship

Still, the commercialism of the Games worries many people. To some, the Olympics today seem to be about money first and everything else—fair play, loyalty, doing one's best—second. "Everyone knows the refrain," a journalist wrote in 1996. "Money is murdering the spirit of sportsmanship."[70] Indeed, the 1996 Atlanta Games came under particular fire for the extent of their commercialization.

Organizers put corporate logos on streetlights, sawhorses, and subway station floors. A McDonald's sign appeared over the edge of the Olympic stadium roof, stationed so that television cameras picked it up during the Parade of Nations. A magazine contained an ad that read, in part: "To the names of [Olympic stars] Jim Thorpe, Bob Mathias, and Rafer Johnson, add the name of Plymouth Voyager."[71] In the opinion of a former Olympian disgusted with Atlanta's corporate hype, "There's no point to the [Games] any more."[72]

There are other, more specific concerns. Some see the influence of television as cause for alarm. Even in 1972, TV helped dictate the schedule of events to maximize viewership in key countries, notably the United States. The men's basketball final at Munich, for instance, began at 11:45 P.M. local time, which was 5:45 P.M. in the eastern United States. Television networks have come under fire, too, for playing up some sports at the expense of others. Coverage of the Winter Games, for example, focuses heavily on figure skating. "A split-level Olympics has emerged," says a journalist, "with the few glamour sports getting all the attention and all the dough, while the other sports go begging."[73] In this view, commercial interests help determine what everybody watches.

While television may be a corrupting influence, corporate sponsorships are potentially more dangerous. With so much money at stake, it is conceivable that a sponsor, rather than a coach, might pick a team or call plays in an attempt to help its investment. In 1992 Nike ran into controversy over just such a situation. U.S. men's track and field coach Mel Rosen had been accepting endorsement money from Nike for many years. At the last minute, he replaced a member of his 4 x 400 relay team with Nike-sponsored runner Michael Johnson, who had not tried to qualify in the individual 400-meter distance. Many observers, including some of the other relay members,

American gold medalist Don Lundquist (right) trades pins with fellow Olympic enthusiasts during the Barcelona Games. As Olympic commercialism expands, critics grow increasingly concerned that corporate sponsorship is corrupting the Olympic spirit.

immediately questioned whether the goal was to field the best possible team—or whether Nike had orchestrated the change to get another pair of Nike shoes on the track in a glamour event the U.S. was likely to win. Although Johnson developed into an outstanding 400 runner, suspicion about Rosen's motives in 1992 remained.

The future

There may not be a repeat of the commercialism that surrounded the Atlanta Games any time soon. The IOC has considered passing rules that will limit corporate involvement, and several bidders to host future Olympics have made it clear that they will not tolerate so many sponsors. For some observers, these steps are all to the good. Some still wish the Games would go further. "Take the brand names off the uniforms, shoes, sunglasses and socks," writes a journalist. "Let the athletes merely advertise themselves, glorious performers stretching human endeavor to its limits."[74]

But other commentators point out that corporate money helps make the Olympics the spectacle that they are. Commercial sponsorships, these people argue, bring the best athletes in the world together at the Games, thereby creating interest that allows the events to be broadcast all across the world. In this view, commercialization is a benefit, not a problem. Moreover, some argue, the whole question of commercialism is overblown. "They said commercialism would kill the Games," writes a reporter. "Hardly. In a world where weapons are sold like hot cakes, who really worries about getting and spending at a sports event?"[75]

Perhaps, in the end, perspective is everything. When a cyclist crosses the finish line or a volleyball crashes to the ground for match point, competitors and audience are typically exulting in the moment, not thinking about sponsorships and corporate cash. A Kentucky newspaper editorial suggests that fans and athletes would do well to keep this truth in mind. "May the TV cameras and endorsement contracts not distract [the competitors] from the real bliss of the Games," the editorial reads: "doing their best against the best in the world."[76]

4

Size and Participation

Of ALL THE sports on the Olympic roster, modern pentathlon may be the most obscure. Designed to simulate the journey of a courier assigned to deliver an important message in wartime, the event consists of five parts that have little in common: fencing, horsemanship, swimming, running, and shooting. The sport is ignored by American television and by the media in most other nations as well. Modern pentathlon news is generally reported only in the smallest possible type in newspaper sports sections. Indeed, it is something of a joke sport. "About 15 people worldwide—most of them out-of-work East German generals—participate in that arcane event, which is about as modern as a wind-up watch," writes a columnist sardonically. "It's expensive, it's time-consuming, and it has no fan base."[77]

But modern pentathlon *has* been in the news lately, though for a reason that does not make its few fans and competitors happy: almost alone among the sports that make up the Summer Games, it has been threatened with extinction by the IOC. The reason is twofold. The sport is unpopular, and the Olympics are growing. Amid worries that the Games are fast becoming unmanageable, some members of the IOC have urged dropping some sports and events. From their perspective, modern pentathlon is a compelling potential target.

Participants hope to keep modern pentathlon on the Olympic program. History is on their side; no sport has been dropped from the Olympics since polo was eliminated in 1936. The pentathlon supporters may yet prevail, but that is by no means certain. It is possible that within the next few Olympiads, modern pentathlon will be dropped from the Games, a victim of the explosive growth of the Olympics.

Growth

There is no doubt that the Games have increased enormously in size over the last several Olympiads. Within the last twenty years, the Summer Olympics have added events including synchronized swimming, tennis, mountain biking, badminton, and beach volleyball. Within the same time span, the Winter Games have seen the arrival of snowboarding,

Canadian Alison Sydor (left) and American Susan Demattei bump handlebars while racing in a mountain-biking competition during the 1996 Altanta Games. Mountain biking is one of many recent additions to the Summer Olympics.

short-track speed skating, curling, moguls, and other new categories. Sports already in the Games are growing, too. Soccer and ice hockey, for instance, are now medal sports for women as well as men, and there are more skiing and yachting races than ever before.

As the events grow, so do the numbers of athletes. The 1896 Olympics drew just over three hundred competitors. By 1924 the figure had reached three thousand; by 1960, five thousand; and by 1988, eight thousand. For the 1996 Atlanta Games, nearly eleven thousand athletes showed up, and early estimates for Sydney in 2000 are larger still. The same sort of growth is evident in figures for the Winter Olympics. The seven hundred athletes who came to the first Winter Games in 1948 had doubled in number for the Calgary Games forty years later. Most recently, twenty-four hundred athletes competed in Nagano during the 1998 Winter Games.

Newcomers

Part of the increase comes from the new events, of course, but some of it comes from the rising popularity of the Games throughout the world. Nations that never sent athletes to the Games are sending them now. This is particularly true of the Winter Games, but the number of nations represented in the Summer Games has jumped from 112 in Mexico City and 159 in Seoul to 197 in Atlanta. Most of the recent entrants have no hopes of winning medals, but their teams swell the ranks of athletes all the same.

To some observers, this growth is all to the good. As the number of medal sports increases, fans of softball, aerial skiing, and table tennis will tune into the Games with greater interest than ever before. One of the goals of the Olympics is participation; this goal is admirably met as the number of athletes participating climbs. Another goal is world harmony, and certainly that ideal is better served when 197 countries enter the Games than when only 112 do. But not everyone believes that growth is healthy for the Olympics. As the debate on modern pentathlon indicates, some members of the IOC have been trying to cut the Olympics down in size. To these influential people—and many members of the media, athletes, and ordinary fans—the Games have become too large, too crowded, and too complicated.

Logistics and the Olympic atmosphere

One problem cited by the IOC is logistical. The way that organizing committees deal with housing, in particular, has changed significantly over the past thirty years. Some IOC members believe that the changes have been far from positive. They argue that host cities simply cannot handle any more athletes—indeed, that they cannot appropriately house the athletes, team officials, and judges that have come to recent Games.

No one denies that Olympic Villages today are much more spread out than they used to be. In 1984 Los Angeles pioneered the concept of using existing housing, mainly college dormitories and the like, and most cities since then have followed suit. The venues, too, are increasingly distant from one another, which has led to some competitors being housed far from the center of the Games. While the 1992 Winter Olympics were based in Albertville, France, about two-thirds of the events were held in other towns. Likewise, the yachting, canoeing, and beach volleyball tournaments were all held miles from Atlanta in 1996. The days of all competitors being in the same place seem to be over.

Despite the numbers, it is still possible to put on a good, efficient Olympics. The careful planning of, say, the 1994 Lillehammer Winter Games clearly demonstrates that. Still, there is no question that the sheer number of athletes makes it much harder to do a passable job. The effects of larger, more spread-out Games go beyond questions of where athletes are to sleep. They include transportation headaches, both for athletes and for fans; administrative issues, as it becomes harder for one central authority to manage the whole area; and ticket problems, as it becomes increasingly hard for fans to find, buy, and sell tickets to events. The more international the Games become, the more complexity is added to even a straightforward task such as meal planning.

But the concerns about size are not simply logistical. Some commentators wonder whether the ideals of the Games are compromised when the number of competitors shoots up. "Isn't the appeal of the Winter Games rooted in a simpler time?"[78] asked a commentator distressed by the sheer number of athletes at the 1998 Nagano Olympics. The spreading venues and villages make it difficult to impart an international flavor to the Games. At Albertville in 1992, "the athletes complained bitterly about the lack of Olympic atmosphere," writes David Wallechinsky, "because they were unable to mingle with athletes from other sports."[79]

Moreover, the number of sports and competitors can tire and overwhelm fans and athletes alike. "I feel like I'm being held prisoner by the television,"[80] complained an American about the Atlanta Games. Fans want to know as much as possible about Olympic events and winners, but nowadays there are too many events for the average fan to follow. The athletes' situation may be even worse. Adding competitors increases the amount of time needed to run events, and adding events strains the schedule at venues. Competitors such as divers, skiers, and middle distance runners can spend all day at their arenas waiting for an event, while some competitions have to be held at times that are awkward for everyone.

"Ridiculous" sports, and others

Several solutions have been proposed to combat the problem of size. The most frequent suggestion is that certain sports be cut from the Olympic roster. The sports proposed for removal vary. Some want to eliminate baseball because it does not currently allow professionals. The survival of ice dancing is questionable because of charges of bias by judges. Weight lifting draws criticism because so many of its athletes are caught using drugs. Others protest boxing because of its violence and cycling because it relies so heavily on technological advances. With respect to equestrian events, one writer asks, "Who deserves the medal, rider or horse?"[81]

A few people have made cases for sweeping entire categories of sports out of the Olympics. Journalist E. M. Swift labels synchronized swimming and rhythmic gymnastics "ridiculous," and urges the removal of both.[82] Another commentator has proposed the elimination of all judged sports on the grounds that they are performances, not true contests of athletic ability. Some reject recent additions like snowboarding and beach volleyball as not traditional enough. Still others object to yachting, shooting, and other sports in which tip-top athletic condition is not necessarily a requirement for doing well. "It is not a sport," writes a Canadian about curling. "It's another excuse to drink beer."[83]

The IOC does not go along with any of these arguments. Its official position, however, is that sports must be popular internationally or risk extinction. Rule 32 states, in part, "Only sports widely practiced by men in at least forty countries and three continents may be included in the program of the Games of the Olympiad"[84]—that is, the Summer Games. (There are somewhat looser requirements for women's sports and the Winter Games.) Yet if Rule 32 were strictly interpreted, it would cause the immediate elimination of quite a few sports, including baseball, canoeing, yachting, fencing, and—as David Wallechinsky points out—"the entire Winter Olympics."[85] It is Rule 32 that is being invoked by those who want to eliminate modern pentathlon.

Finally, a few observers argue that certain events, rather than whole sports, should be dropped. Wrestling weight classes, for instance, could be reworked. Instead of establishing weight limits five or six kilograms apart, the IOC could widen the spans to ten kilograms and thus do away with several competitions. As for track? "Drop some events," advises a track fan. "Cut their number by as much as half. Get rid of those that allow doubling up"—the events so similar in demands that the same person often wins.[86]

However, with the possible exception of modern pentathlon, it seems very doubtful that any sport will be dropped entirely any time soon. Every sport currently in the Games has a following, if only a small one, and fans and competitors would object if their sport were eliminated. So would officials. "Judges won't go easily," sighs a reporter, explaining why a ban on judged sports would probably fail. "They seldom pass the death sentence upon themselves."[87]

Why sports stay

Rule 32 notwithstanding, the IOC retains sports for reasons other than simple popularity. Various events please people whom the IOC would like to attract or—at the very least—not offend. Snowboarding may strike one fan as a silly sport that "makes as much sense [in the Olympics] as having the best pinball players in the world gather in

Members of Canada's curling team compete in the 1998 Winter Games. As the Olympics continue to add new events to its schedule, critics have suggested that outdated and unpopular competitions, including curling, should be eliminated.

Sydney in 2000,"[88] but snowboarding is very popular in some places and especially appeals to younger fans. Similarly, some women's events, notably ice hockey, do not approach the popularity standards called for by the IOC, but the guidelines were waived in the interest of the greater goal of providing more opportunities for female athletes.

Nor does it seem likely that cutting events will greatly reduce the number of competitors. When the IOC did eliminate a few swimming relays briefly in the 1970s, most of the swimmers who would have participated were entered in individual events as well. Thus, there was no net change in the number of athletes. Synchronized swimming actually increased the number of competitors even as it reduced its events from two to one; the two events dropped were solo and duet competitions, while the addition was an eight-member team event. As for track and field, sports officials have let it be known that they will not stand for much trimming. "If they try to cut athletics [track and field] down in the Olympic Games," threatened a recent president of track and field's international governing body, "we will simply leave the Olympics altogether."[89]

Finally, despite the IOC's apparent interest in cutting sports, the addition of new ones is continuing. Tae kwon do and triathlon will join the program in Sydney. Other sports are knocking at the IOC's door, too. Potential candidates for future Olympics include bowling, jai alai, surfing, and a cross between basketball and team handball known as korfball. Even ballroom dancing is building a case. If decisions are to be consistent with the IOC's stated concern about the size of the Olympics, it is unlikely that any of these sports will be admitted to the Games. But based on what IOC members have done in the recent past, it seems quite likely that at least one or two of these events will be on a future Olympics schedule.

Sports tourism

If cutting sports and events is not a possibility, then perhaps the number of competitors can be reduced. "Cut out preliminary rounds,"[90] urges one observer. Instead of inviting several dozen runners to compete in the glamorous track events and eliminating them gradually in heats, just bring in the very best athletes and have them compete in an immediate "final." The idea behind this proposal makes sense to many fans. Fewer competitors would mean fewer stresses on the host city and fewer scheduling headaches at the track.

The idea of eliminating competitors seems especially compelling to opponents of so-called sports tourism. "Sports tourists" are athletes, usually from small nations, who have no chance of winning a medal but who compete anyhow. There are dozens of examples from Olympic history. In 1976 a Haitian runner finished the men's 10,000-meter run in 42 minutes—almost 15 minutes after the winner and more than 8 minutes after the next-to-last finisher. During the 1992 Winter Games, a Costa Rican skier completed two runs of the slalom event in a combined time of just over 4 minutes 29 seconds; the winner's total, in contrast, was 1:44. The Costa Rican, wrote an observer, "seemed to walk down the mountain, testing each step like a bather putting his bare foot into freezing water."[91]

Sports tourism has been controversial. The IOC has encouraged it, allowing athletes from some smaller nations to compete at the Games even if they do not meet international qualifying standards. In some cases, the IOC foots the bill for a poor nation to send its athletes, no matter how unprepared they might be for competition at the Olympic level. Support for this policy comes from nations that lack the necessary resources to train athletes But support also comes from those who believe the Games are about participation. "There's a great opportunity for friendships," says a Canadian Olympic official. "There's room for everyone."[92]

It is also true that the weaker competitors often add color and drama to the Olympics. Viewers often thrill to the sight of a lone athlete, from a country many people could not locate on a map, proudly bearing his or her national flag in the opening parade. And a few of these also-rans become celebrities: witness the Jamaican bobsledders, whose story was turned into the movie *Cool Runnings*, or

Great Britain's Eddie "the Eagle" Edwards, the country's only competitor in the ski jump, placed last in the 1988 Winter Games but won the hearts of many spectators.

the ungainly Eddie "the Eagle" Edwards, a British ski jumper at the Calgary Games. "He was not the best ski jumper that ever took to the hill, but I remember Eddie," one fan wrote ten years later. "I couldn't tell you who did win the gold or silver that year."[93]

Others, however, feel that sports tourists simply do not belong in the Games. "The Olympic movement doesn't want athletes taking a free ride [to the Olympics] if they shouldn't be in the competition,"[94] said an IOC official the year before the Calgary Games. In this view, athletes who are less than world class at their sports are an embarrassment to the Olympics. Such athletes use up precious resources, too; in one case, a distance runner took so long to complete his event that heats for the next race had to be delayed. To address some of these concerns, the IOC has found small ways of making certain that events are not disrupted by the number of participants. Any road race cyclist who falls a certain distance behind the main pack, for example, is now made to leave the course.

"Bureaucrats and hangers-on"

Other proposals have been made to reduce the stresses on cities that host the Games. Leonard Koppett suggests that the Games be further broken up, just as the Winter and Summer Games are today. During an Olympic year, all sports would get their turn, but at different times. "Skiing in January," he writes, "skating and hockey in February, team sports in June, water sports in July, track and field in August, gymnastics in October—some such pattern would work like a charm."[95] Or the Games could be dispersed geographically, much as was done in Albertville only even more so; while no Olympic festival has been awarded yet based on a two- or three-city proposal, several bidders have proposed exactly that scenario. David Wallechinsky suggests that the IOC cut down on the number of team officials allowed. "The roster of Olympic participants is bloated with bureaucrats and hangers-on,"[96] he charges.

These changes appear unlikely any time soon. Expanding the Games, either by extending events over a longer period of time or by spreading them across a larger area, might solve logistical problems but would present other difficulties. Spreading competitions throughout the year might diminish the impact of the Games. As for giving the Games to several cities at once, that would work against the Olympic goal of bringing athletes together from across the world. Rather than a huge festival encompassing athletes from all sports and dozens of countries, the Games might increasingly seem like just another meet, race, or contest, without anything special to recommend them. The issue of size, in the end, comes down to three questions: one practical and two philosophical.

Question of size

First, and perhaps most important: Can the Olympics succeed in housing, feeding, and managing the number of athletes who show up every four years? The evidence on this question is mixed. The 1992 Albertville Winter Games have often been cited as a logistical disappointment; the 1994 Games of Lillehammer, in contrast, were applauded for their attention to detail. The best hope for success may lie in lead time: the IOC awards Games six years in advance—a period that may be long enough to allow the hosts to work out every scheduling kink and housing dilemma, no matter how many athletes are expected.

Second, is overcoming the logistical problems worth the effort? As the Games grow, that growth must inevitably change the way they are run. Something may be lost when athletes are housed far from competitors in other sports. Something else may be lost when they spend more time on the bus than in the Olympic Village and more time waiting for other events to end than taking part in their own. The advantages of having extra sports and exotic performers may not outweigh the disadvantages that could come with size.

Performers in Atlanta's crowded Olympic Stadium celebrate the centennial of the Summer Games. As the international competition enters its next century, its organizers will try to maintain the integrity of the games in light of growing commercialism and expansion.

Finally, the third question may be the most basic of all: Are Olympic ideals better met by encouraging participation or by encouraging excellence? Coubertin's original notion was that participation was more important. In his vision, the Olympics were not a forum for the world's best athletes so much as a forum for international understanding and brotherhood. In most cases, the two goals are not in conflict—but in some areas, such as keeping the Olympics to a manageable size, they are.

Those who believe that excellence is the key are likely to worry about the size of the Games. For them, too many athletes, too many events, and too many obscure sports detract from the essence of the Olympics. On the other hand, those who see participation as most important do not care much about the size of the Olympics. Indeed, for them, bigger may truly be better. How the next generation of IOC officials chooses to answer this question will determine the direction the Games will take.

5

Drugs

THE MEN'S 100-METER dash has never been more visible than it was during the 1988 Seoul Games. That year, Canadian sprinter Ben Johnson jumped out to a quick lead and never looked back on his way to the gold medal. He broke the world record and finished thirteen hundredths of a second before anyone else. It was a major upset of favored American Carl Lewis, and Canadians rejoiced. A headline in a Toronto newspaper referred to Johnson as a national treasure. Johnson basked in the glory. The companies that had already signed him to commercial deals gloated, and others rushed to sign him up.

But the joy was short-lived. Before he could be formally certified as Olympic champion, Johnson—like nearly all medalists—had to submit to a urine test designed to determine whether he was using drugs banned by the IOC. The IOC tests hundreds of urine samples every Olympics, and only a handful turn out positive. Johnson's was one that did. His urine showed clear traces of stanozolol, a drug on the IOC's forbidden list. A day and a half after the medals ceremony, a Canadian Olympic representative came to collect Johnson's gold medal, which would be given instead to Lewis, the runner-up. "We love you," the representative told Johnson, "but you're guilty."[97]

At first Johnson denied any drug use. Indeed, his coach suggested that the urine sample or Johnson's water bottle had somehow been sabotaged by supporters of Carl Lewis. But the Canadian government started a judicial inquiry into the taking of banned substances by its athletes, and the

Canada's Ben Johnson sprints to the finish in the 100-meter race, clinching the gold medal. Just days later Johnson was stripped of his medal after testing positive for steroid use.

truth came out. Johnson's coach and doctor had been feeding him steroid pills for seven years. Apparently the coach had convinced Johnson that every other competitor took steroids and there would be no possibility of keeping up without them.

The Johnson saga is a sad one in many ways. Johnson's drug use destroyed his credibility and his career, and the long-term effects on his health are unknown. After serving a two-year suspension, Johnson returned to the track, only to be permanently banned in 1993 following another positive drug test in a non-Olympic competition. But Johnson's decision to use performance-enhancing drugs has affected the Olympics themselves as well. Drug use by such a visible and successful competitor has brought up questions concerning the prevalence of chemicals in the Games. It has also led to increased debate over what can, should, and must be done to make sure that drugs do not destroy the health of athletes, devalue Olympic medals, and corrupt the vision of the Games as a contest between the best athletes—not the best pharmacists—of the world.

From strychnine to steroids—and beyond

Almost since the beginning of the Olympics, competitors have ingested drugs and other materials intended to boost their performances. The 1904 marathon winner, Thomas Hicks, swallowed a mixture of brandy and strychnine— a chemical used in rat poison—while running. Somewhat later, the use of amphetamines became popular, especially in endurance sports such as cycling. During the 1960 cycling road race in Rome, one competitor, Knut Jensen of Denmark, collapsed and died; it was later discovered that his death was partly due to amphetamines he had taken just before the race.

However, drug use increased dramatically during the 1950s and 1960s with the discovery that a class of drugs called steroids—including stanozolol—might help athletes build muscle, speed, and endurance. Word spread quickly through the Olympic community. "By the 1960s," one observer reports, "it was virtually a given that nearly all world-class weight lifters used steroids."[98] The IOC was slow to react. It did not formally ban performance-enhancing drugs until 1968, waited until 1972 to institute full-scale testing, and did not ban steroid use until 1976—partly because no firm test for steroids had been developed before 1974.

By then, drug use in the Games was well entrenched. U.S. hammer thrower Harold Connolly spoke of athletes in the 1968 Mexico City Games who had "so many puncture holes from injected drugs that it was difficult to find a fresh injection site."[99] Throughout the 1960s and 1970s, the East German government required its athletes, male and female alike, to take steroids—often without telling them

YOU CAN RUN BUT YOU CAN'T HIDE

what the drugs were. In 1972 American competitor Jay Sylvester asked his colleagues on the U.S. track and field team whether they had taken steroids. Though track's governing body had banned steroids two years earlier, two-thirds of Sylvester's teammates reported having used them within the preceding six months.

Since 1972 new drugs have appeared, taking their place alongside steroids. Some athletes have been caught using testosterone, a male hormone that is needed for normal development in both men and women. Though it occurs natu-

American hammer thrower Harold Connolly, shown here competing in the 1956 Olympics in Melbourne, Australia, confirmed reports of drug use by athletes in the 1968 Mexico City Games.

rally in the body, some competitors inject themselves with testosterone in the belief that it will give them an extra edge. Another natural chemical, known simply as human growth hormone, has recently been isolated in the laboratory. While its medical use is limited to people who are unusually short, human growth hormone fetches a very high price on the black market among athletes. And a substance called erythropoietin, or EPO for short, is in demand because of its ability to increase the oxygen-carrying capabilities of the blood. All these drugs are known to Olympic athletes, and all are banned by the IOC.

Health hazards

While these substances may indeed improve athletic performance, they all carry extremely serious health risks. Steroids, for instance, can cause sterility in both women and men. Women who use steroids often develop male characteristics such as beards and deep voices. Possible effects on men include enlarged breasts and shrunken testicles. Long-term effects are perhaps more frightening. Kidney and liver disease, increased risk of heart attacks, and certain cancers are among diseases linked with high steroid use. "Young athletes who take heavy doses of anabolic steroids for 60 to 90 days," says one physician, "should expect to die in their 30s or 40s."[100]

Both men and women can suffer psychological damage from steroids, too. Former users often say that steroid use gave them a feeling of invulnerability, leading some to drive recklessly or engage in other dangerous behaviors. Most users become irritable, and many go into violent episodes known informally as "'roid rages." While some of the physical and psychological effects related to steroids diminish if an athlete stops using the drug, others are permanent.

Other substances are problematic as well. EPO has been blamed for the deaths of at least two dozen cyclists, some of them Olympians. The long-term effects of human growth hormone in high doses are almost entirely unknown, particularly where people of normal stature are concerned. Amphetamines, as mentioned, were implicated

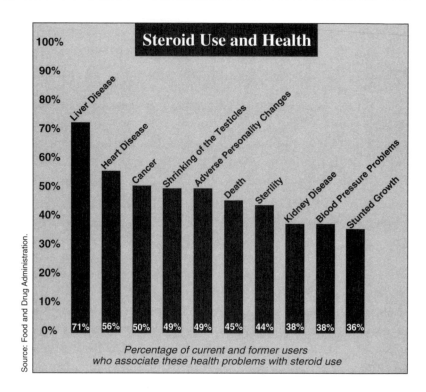

Steroid Use and Health

Liver Disease — 71%
Heart Disease — 56%
Cancer — 50%
Shrinking of the Testicles — 49%
Adverse Personality Changes — 49%
Death — 45%
Sterility — 44%
Kidney Disease — 38%
Blood Pressure Problems — 38%
Stunted Growth — 36%

*Percentage of current and former users
who associate these health problems with steroid use*

Source: Food and Drug Administration.

in the death of cyclist Knut Jensen in Rome. The wisdom of using any of these drugs is highly questionable.

A procedure called blood boosting is another dangerous means of artificially enhancing athletic performance. Blood boosting involves injecting a quart of blood shortly before a competition, thus raising the level of oxygen-carrying red blood cells. Some athletes begin stockpiling their own blood months before a major competition, while others use donated blood. Blood boosting can be the source of deadly infections such as HIV and hepatitis B; it has also caused kidney damage. Results for athletes who used the technique in Los Angeles in 1984 were mixed. While several U.S. cyclists won gold medals after blood boosting, two others became sick. "[I] rode the worst I ever rode in my life,"[101] one said afterward.

The Olympic charter forbids use of any of the "performance-enhancing" drugs, including—since 1984—the practice of blood boosting. Indeed, the IOC currently bans literally dozens of substances, ranging from steroids and lab-generated testosterone all the way down to certain cold medicines, many pain relievers, and even certain herbal teas. Anything that might give a competitor an unfair edge is forbidden. The list is so long and complex that the IOC advises athletes to check with team doctors before taking any medication whatsoever.

"The single biggest threat"

Very few athletes have been caught using banned drugs at the Olympics. Ben Johnson appears at the head of a rather short list. No Olympiad has ever seen more than twelve competitors banned after positive drug tests, and nearly all the positive samples belonged to nonmedalists. At first glance, that statistic suggests that drugs are not a significant issue in the Olympics. However, even the most optimistic observers admit that failure rates are not a good indicator of the degree of drug use.

Just how widespread drug use is among Olympians is a matter of some debate. "Only 15 percent of [Olympic] athletes take drugs," says Christiane Ayotte, a Canadian drug expert. "No more than that, I'm sure."[102] Still, 15 percent is close to one in seven, far more than the drug test failure rate would indicate, and most observers fear that Ayotte's estimate is far too low. "I would say nearly every top-level athlete is on something,"[103] says Michael Mooney,

a bodybuilder who says he has advised elite competitors on how to avoid detection. Others who believe that a significant majority of serious competitors dope include Olympic athletes in sports such as cycling, track, and weight lifting; Emil Vrijman, the head of the Netherlands doping control center; and Dr. Robert Voy, the USOC's chief medical officer during the 1980s. "Drugs are the single biggest threat to the Games,"[104] concludes writer Gary Allison.

Why have Olympic tests revealed so few drug users? The answer lies partly with the testing process itself. The screening procedure used during the Olympics relies on urine tests to detect drug use, but these procedures are often flawed. The equipment is sensitive, to be sure: sensitive enough to detect a sugar cube dissolved in a swimming pool. But even that sensitivity is not enough to capture very small amounts of very powerful substances. Traces of some steroids, moreover, disappear from the body overnight. EPO and human growth hormone cannot be detected by urine tests under any circumstances.

Worse, cheating on a urine test is quite easy, according to athletes who have done it. A common method is passing off someone else's urine as one's own. This is more difficult now that Olympic protocol requires that an official watch the competitor urinate, but it can be done. Some female competitors, for example, have concealed urine-filled balloons in their vaginas, then broken them to produce a sample; men have been known to inject "clean" urine into their bladders before their events.

It is also possible to evade detection by using another substance to hide, or mask, the drug. Drinking certain herbal teas or liquids containing high quantities of vinegar may cover traces of some chemicals. Some competitors also take diuretics—drugs that make the user urinate frequently—in an effort to rid their bodies of traces of steroids. Like steroids, diuretics carry health risks, notably the chance of dehydration, and other masking agents have different unpleasant effects when used in large quantities. Because of the dangers and the possibility that some athletes will use these drugs only to help make a urine test negative, diuretics and other masking agents are banned by the IOC as well.

Given all the possible ways of cheating, some observers adopt a pessimistic point of view. Testing "can't, and never will, catch everyone," says an Olympic official. "The best we can hope for is that regular testing will lead to a decrease in drug use."[105] Others, however, say that the situation is not nearly so bleak. Better, more accurate, tests can be developed, they argue. Cheating can be contained by using new, more thorough ways of administering the tests. In the long run, they believe, drug use among Olympic athletes can be stopped. In 1996, for instance, the IOC bought three state-of-the-art testing machines to deploy in Atlanta. The cost—$700,000 apiece—pointed toward the IOC's determination to run a clean Games.

High technology

Unfortunately, to some extent the scientific advances have helped the drug users more than the IOC. "It's like a cat-and-mouse game with testers and cheaters," one expert says. "Whoever has the highest technology wins."[106] Athletes now can use science and medicine, for instance, to determine which doses of which drugs can be taken on which days to escape detection. Finnigan MAT, the company that makes the $700,000 machines, sells about thirty of these devices every year. Even the company admits that some, if not most, of the machines sold are used to help athletes beat the IOC's machines by determining what combinations of drugs and doses will register positive tests—and which will not.

Drug testers are also faced with the problem of so-called designer drugs. These are substances that have been chemically altered so that they no longer match the exact description of the drugs testers are looking for. "The sophisticated athlete," admits a U.S. lab director, "has switched to things we can't test for."[107] A recent example is the drug bromantan, developed by Russian scientists as a way of keeping soldiers alert in extreme weather conditions. Several eastern European athletes were suspended from the Atlanta

A doctor in a Barcelona laboratory examines athletes' test samples during the 1992 Olympic Games. Despite intensive testing, some new high-tech drugs are undetectable by officials.

Games for using bromantan. In the end, however, their medals were returned to them. Though bromantan may well have been worthy of banning, the IOC had not expressly banned it before 1996. (It has now.) Once again, the health risks of taking bromantan are essentially unknown. "There are no clinical studies with this substance," warns a researcher, "no toxicity studies, nothing."[108]

For substances that occur naturally, the IOC has developed other means of detection. Testosterone, for instance, is found in both men and women. The IOC has developed tables showing the approximate amount expected in an athlete's body, depending on weight and gender. Because there is normal variation from person to person—and even from one week to the next in an individual—the amounts are set high enough to allow for those variations. That amount of leeway makes it difficult to determine who has "unnaturally" high levels of testosterone and leads to inconsistent enforcement of the rules. Of two 1996 U.S. Olympians with excessive testosterone levels, for instance, Sandra Farmer-Patrick was given a four-year suspension, while Mary Decker Slaney was not punished. Despite the complications, however, most observers applaud the IOC for establishing guidelines for catching testosterone users.

Solutions

One possible answer to cheating on drug tests is the institution of random tests. With such unscheduled screening, Olympic Committees and governing bodies of individual sports can test a competitor for drugs at any moment they choose. A positive result would mean a suspension, possibly through the next Olympics. In theory, awareness that a system of random tests is in place should keep athletes honest. But not all sports and nations permit random testing, in part because the practice raises privacy and civil liberties questions. Moreover, some doctors and trainers boast that they can devise a drug program that will not show up even under random testing. "No athlete I've ever helped has tested positive, and I've helped hundreds,"[109] says a Dutch physician. Still, there is no doubt that random testing makes it hard for athletes to use drugs of certain types without detection.

Blood tests are another possibility. Many banned chemicals that leave no traces in urine will show up in the blood. Consequently, there is some thought of instituting blood tests in time for the Sydney Games. Unfortunately, blood tests have drawbacks too. They are far more expensive to administer than urine tests. The technology, though powerful, is new and therefore suspect. Besides, says steroids expert Bob Goldman, "blood's too much of a pain. Blood spoils. Tubes break. . . . People pass out."[110] Of course, some of the same complaints were made prior to the introduction of urine testing, so blood testing may yet have a future in the Games.

Finally, some observers point to the athletes who do not dope as the best chance for honesty in the Games. Some Olympic competitors, such as Carl Lewis and U.S. swimmer Janet Evans, have been vocal in their support for testing measures and have lent their names to many antidoping messages. Unfortunately, not all athletes can take those messages to heart. Rightly or wrongly, many competitors have heard from their coaches what Ben Johnson heard from his: that cheating was necessary to win. "The pressure to take drugs is enormous," says a U.S. shot-putter. "An athlete asks himself, 'Do I take drugs and win medals, or do I play fair and finish last?'"[111] Nevertheless, strong stands by respected and victorious athletes can help tremendously in the battle against drugs.

Indeed, the stigma associated with using drugs is great. For a few hours Ben Johnson was the toast of Seoul. Then his urine test came up positive, and he left the city in disgrace, his credibility gone and with it the respect of the world. Simply the accusation of doping can damage an athlete's reputation, and those who have failed tests are often scorned by teammates and opponents alike. "It's like being accused of child molesting," says Mary Decker Slaney's coach, referring to the test that revealed Slaney's high testosterone level. "Just [publicizing the story] is [bad] enough, even when it's not true."[112] However widespread doping may be, it is far from acceptable behavior, at least according to fans, media, and the corporations that help underwrite the Games and their athletes. "I've got a gut feeling that some sponsors feel funny about sponsoring druggies,"[113] remarks an IOC member.

Lawsuits, contamination, and sabotage

Because of the stigma and the possibility of suspension, most competitors who are accused of doping fight the results to the bitter end. Some charge accidental contamination of their samples. Ben Johnson, for instance, appealed his lifetime ban on the grounds that his urine may not have been kept at a constant temperature. Other competitors charge sabotage. Belgian runner Ria van Landeghem missed the Seoul Olympics because Belgian authorities found "substantial" amounts of steroids in a urine test administered just before her event.[114] Van Landeghem had a long history of conflict with the Belgian Olympic committee; she has voiced the suspicion that Belgian officials may have tampered with her sample.

Increasingly, perhaps in part to avoid lawsuits, the IOC and its member committees are ruling in favor of athletes who claim sabotage or human error. Hurdler Ludmila Engquist, a Russian now competing for Sweden, was originally suspended for steroid use, but when her former husband admitted he had spiked her protein supplement in hopes that she would be caught, her suspension was reduced. Engquist went on to win a gold medal in Atlanta. U.S. swimmer Jessica Foschi was reinstated in 1996 after authorities determined that a sample had indeed been sabotaged—by whom no one knows. Even in these cases, however, competitors lose valuable time and reputations are tarnished.

"It turns off the public"

Some observers charge that Olympic officials do not always push hard enough for drug testing. There is some evidence to support this. All pre-Olympic testing is left up to national foundations, but most national Olympic Committees do not enforce a standard of testing as rigorous as the one developed for the IOC. Only three nations—Germany,

Canada, and Japan—are noted for taking testing seriously. Other nations lack the resources or the will to spend money to combat the problem.

The United States likes to point fingers at nations such as Russia and China where doping is concerned, but in fact many offenders have been Americans. Until quite recently USOC testing was largely confined to tests just before competitors were to leave for the Olympics. "You only look at a team before it leaves to make sure it doesn't get caught,"[115] charges a Canadian drug control expert. In this view, the U.S. goal has been to make sure it is not obliged to forfeit medals at the Games, rather than to identify drug-taking athletes out of concern for their health and future, and for the integrity of the Olympics.

Moreover, the United States has often been reluctant to accept positive tests relating to its own athletes. When Olympic track and field medalists Dennis Mitchell and Randy Barnes failed out-of-competition tests in 1998, their international federation immediately suspended them. Craig Masback, the director of USA Track and Field, released a statement saying, in part, that his organization "objects to the . . . suspensions and will not enforce them."[116] While the suspensions may have been prematurely announced, Masback's comments reinforced the notion that the United States was refusing to acknowledge drug use among its own athletes. Such accusations have been leveled at other countries, as well.

Finally, some question how badly Olympic officials want to find cheaters. During Ben Johnson's steroids trial it was revealed that the IOC often covered up or refused to pursue clear evidence of drug use. "The IOC fears exposing the high levels of drug use," says Dr. Robert Voy, the USOC's director of drug testing during the 1980s. "It turns off the public."[117] Part of the appeal of

During Ben Johnson's trial, a lawyer questions the sprinter about his drug use. The trial also disclosed that the IOC occasionally mishandled drug abuse claims in an effort to prevent the public from learning the actual amount of abuse that occurs in the Games.

the Olympics lies in the notion that the athletes are ordinary human beings pushing themselves to new limits. "Why in the world would . . . hundreds of millions of people choose to watch a competition in which the race goes not to the swift but to the chemically enhanced?"[118] asks the *New York Times*.

The value of testing

All this controversy begs the question: Is testing worth it? A minority of observers says no. Some say that if testing cannot be performed with consistent accuracy, it should be dropped. Others worry that singling a drug out can backfire by making it popular among competitors seeking an edge. Putting a drug on a forbidden list "tells the athlete that this drug improves performance, or we wouldn't ban it," points out the head of testing in the Netherlands.[119] Still others draw no distinction between steroids and other devices intended to improve performance. "Many of the means and ends which athletes use and seek are unnatural," writes Norman Fost, a professor of bioethics. "From Nautilus machines to . . . Gatorade, their lives are filled with drugs and devices whose aim is to maximize performance."[120]

Certainly, many observers believe that the IOC's restrictions and procedures need revision. Even IOC's president Juan Antonio Samaranch has stated that "the actual list of [banned] products must be reduced drastically."[121] Samaranch has suggested, in particular, that the key to branding a drug illegal might be whether it harms an athlete's health. Some argue that the IOC is overzealous in pursuing drugs that must be taken in huge quantities to boost performance. Others question why many drugs, like bromantan, are banned even though no one knows precisely how, or indeed whether, they affect an athlete's health or performance.

But most observers could not disagree more with Samaranch's words. Many experts feel that the answer to widespread doping is not to condone it, and not to accept it, and certainly not to give in to it. Instead, they argue, the Olympics must remain vigilant. That means continuing to try to catch up with the drug designers. It means spending money on new tests and new machines, even instituting blood testing if necessary. It means requiring all sports federations to go along with IOC drug restrictions and testing; as of this writing, tennis, volleyball, and cycling do not. "There has to be a very strong case against a sport that can't produce clean athletes,"[122] says an IOC member from Australia, who questions whether cycling, in particular, should be permitted in the 2000 Games if it does not change its stance.

Vigilance means more, too. It means continuing to isolate and remove wrongdoers, regardless of the outcry from the public or the national sports federations. It means constantly pointing out the health risks of drug use—the men who have died from EPO, the women unknowingly made infertile by steroids, the athletes who have been stricken in their youth by cancers, heart problems, and kidney infections. And above all, vigilance means not giving ground. "I fell under the table when I heard [Samaranch's suggestion]," said Wildor Hollmann, the honorary president of the World Association for Sports Medicine. "That way of thinking is nonsense. That would be an unbelievable step backwards."[123] Most observers agree.

Willing to pay any price

The stakes in the war on drugs are high, both in terms of health and in terms of the integrity of the Olympics. A poll of aspiring American Olympians taken every two years or so demonstrates the depth of the problem. Suppose, the question asks, you could take a substance that would be against the rules of your sport. It would be completely undetectable and would make you a guaranteed Olympic champion; but it would kill you within five years. Would you take it? In poll after poll, over half the athletes say they would. To a competitor bound and determined to win Olympic gold, the answer is clear. Health risks are not even considered. "If I'd told people back then that rat manure would make them strong," says a doctor who advised an Olympic U.S. weight lifting team in the 1960s, "they'd have eaten rat manure."[124] Without some form of drug testing, this argument runs, athletes will even choose to destroy their health in search of a gold medal.

But beyond the health risks, drugs turn the Olympics into an event very far from what Pierre de Coubertin imagined. The Olympics were intended to be a competition between the very best athletes in the world. Even today, that notion is central to the appeal of the Games. The use of drugs degrades that competition into a competition between labs. Where drugs are concerned, the IOC must find a way to return the Olympics to their original conception. This effort will result in restoring the purity of the Games, protecting the health of Olympic competitors, and encouraging fair and natural competition between the best athletes of the world.

Appendix

The Modern Olympic Games

Year	Summer Site	Countries Represented	Winter Site	Countries Represented
1896	Athens, Greece	13		
1900	Paris, France	22		
1904	St. Louis, Missouri, U.S.A.	13		
1906*	Athens	20		
1908	London, England	22	**	6
1912	Stockholm, Sweden	28		
1916	***			
1920	Antwerp, Belgium	29	**	9
1924	Paris	44	Chamonix, France	16
1928	Amsterdam, the Netherlands	46	St. Moritz, Switzerland	25
1932	Los Angeles, California, U.S.A.	37	Lake Placid, New York, U.S.A.	17
1936	Berlin, Germany	49	Garmisch-Partenkirchen, Germany	28
1940	***		***	
1944	***		***	
1948	London	59	St. Moritz	28
1952	Helsinki, Finland	69	Oslo, Norway	30
1956	Melbourne, Australia	71	Cortina, Italy	32
1960	Rome, Italy	83	Squaw Valley, California, U.S.A.	30
1964	Tokyo, Japan	93	Innsbruck, Austria	36
1968	Mexico City, Mexico	112	Grenoble, France	37
1972	Munich, West Germany	122	Sapporo, Japan	35
1976	Montreal, Quebec, Canada	92	Innsbruck****	37
1980	Moscow, Soviet Union	81	Lake Placid	37
1984	Los Angeles	140	Sarajevo, Yugoslavia	49

1988	Seoul, South Korea	159	Calgary, Alberta, Canada	57
1992	Barcelona, Spain	172	Albertville, France	64
1994	*****		Lillehammer, Norway	67
1996	Atlanta, Georgia, U.S.A.	197		
1998			Nagano, Japan	83
2000	Sydney, Australia			
2002			Salt Lake City, Utah, U.S.A.	
2004	Athens			

*The 1906 Games, which marked the tenth anniversary of the 1896 Games, are included in the official record books despite being out of the standard four-year cycle.

**The 1908 Summer Games included figure skating events. The 1920 Summer Games included figure skating and ice hockey.

***Three Summer and two Winter Olympics were canceled because of war. The 1916 Games had been awarded to Berlin; the 1940 Games, first slated for Tokyo, then were set for Helsinki before being abandoned; the 1944 Games had been set for London. The 1940 Winter Games went to Sapporo, then St. Moritz, and then Garmisch-Partenkirchen before being canceled. The 1944 Winter Games had been scheduled for Cortina. All these cities hosted Olympics before or afterward.

****These Games were originally awarded to Denver, Colorado, but voters turned down a proposal to host them before they got under way. Innsbruck agreed to take on the task at the last minute.

*****In 1994 the Olympics moved to a staggered schedule for Summer and Winter Games. To make the change, there were only two years between the 1992 and 1994 Winter Olympics.

Notes

Chapter 1: Professionals and Amateurs

1. Quoted in David Wallechinsky, *The Complete Book of the Olympics*. Woodstock, NY: Overlook Press, 1996, p. 164.

2. Quoted in David Cort, "The Myth of the Amateur," *Nation*, September 28, 1964, p. 158.

3. Richard D. Mandell, *The First Modern Olympics*. Berkeley: University Press of California, 1976, p. 144.

4. Quoted in Richard Grenier, "Olympic Myths," *National Review*, July 29, 1996, p. 52.

5. Quoted in Roger Kahn, "Let's Pull Out of the Olympics," *Saturday Evening Post*, October 10, 1964, p. 10.

6. Quoted in Geoffrey Miller, *Behind the Olympic Rings*. Lynn, MA: H. O. Zimman, 1976, pp. 60–61.

7. Quoted in Miller, *Behind the Olympic Rings*, p. 61.

8. Kahn, "Let's Pull Out of the Olympics," p. 10.

9. Quoted in David Wallechinsky, *The Complete Book of the Winter Olympics, 1998*. Woodstock, NY: Overlook Press, 1998, p. 159.

10. Cort, "The Myth of the Amateur," p. 158.

11. Kahn, "Let's Pull Out of the Olympics," p. 10.

12. Frank McCoy, "Should the Chariots of Fire Be for Hire?" *Business Week*, September 26, 1988, p. 70.

13. *Toledo Blade*, April 16, 1989, quoted in Oliver Trager, ed., *Sports in America: Paradise Lost?* New York: Facts On File, 1990, p. 164.

14. tcspts, "Athletes Behaving Badly" forum, *New York Times Forums*, post #530, February 20, 1998, www.nytimes.com.

15. Fred Zahradnik, "The Pro Invasion," *Bicycling*, June 1996, p. 38.

16. Quoted in Daniel Benjamin, "Pro vs. Amateur," *Time*, July 27, 1992, p. 65.

17. *Hartford Courant*, October 4, 1988, quoted in Trager, ed., *Sports in America*, p. 165.

18. Quoted in Janet Podell, ed., *Sports in America*. New York: H. W. Wilson, 1986, p. 150.

19. Quoted in Wallechinsky, *The Complete Book of the Olympics*, p. 269.

20. Quoted in McCoy, "Should the Chariots of Fire Be for Hire?" p. 70.

21. Roger Angell, "Gold, Silver, Bronze, Irony," *New Yorker*, July 22, 1996, p. 5.

Chapter 2: Politics in the Games

22. Quoted in Jimmy Carter, "Statement from Former U.S. President Jimmy Carter on the 1980 Boycott," March 25, 1996, http://www.cc.emory.edu/CARTER_CENTER/RLS96/olym1980.htm.

23. Quoted in Kenny Moore, "The Pawns Make a Move," *Sports Illustrated*, February 4, 1980, p. 22.

24. Quoted in *People Online's Olympic Heroes*, "Sebastian Coe," http://www.pathfinder.com/people/sp/olympics/coe.html.

25. Quoted in Felix Rosenthal, "Warm Days in Moscow," *Sports Illustrated*, February 4, 1980, p. 25.

26. Wallechinsky, *The Complete Book of the Olympics*, p. xxi.

27. Quoted in Ron Fimrite, "Facing Bear Facts," *Sports Illustrated*, February 4, 1980, p. 21.

28. Quoted in Fimrite, "Facing Bear Facts," p. 21.

29. Quoted in Fimrite, "Facing Bear Facts," p. 21.

30. Quoted in Mandell, *The First Modern Olympics*, p. 72.

31. Mandell, *The First Modern Olympics*, p. 9.

32. Quoted in Mandell, *The First Modern Olympics*, p. 72.

33. Quoted in Miller, *Behind the Olympic Rings*, p. 195.

34. Fred Coleman, "Nationalism: When the Cheering Stops," *U.S. News & World Report*, February 28, 1994, p. 6.

35. David Cort, "The Hungarian Olympics," *Nation*, November 24, 1956, p. 454.

36. Roger Rosenblatt, "Why We Play These Games," in Podell, ed., *Sports in America*, p. 141.

37. Quoted in Cort, "The Hungarian Olympics," p. 454.

38. John Kieran and Arthur Daley, *The Story of the Olympic Games*. Philadelphia: Lippincott, 1961, p. 288.

39. Quoted in Miller, *Behind the Olympic Rings*, photographs following page 238.

40. Quoted in Wallechinsky, *The Complete Book of the Olympics*, p. 297.

41. Quoted in Kieran and Daley, *The Story of the Olympic Games*, p. 316.

42. Rosenblatt, "Why We Play These Games," p. 141.

43. Bob Ottum, "Only You, Mary Lou," *Sports Illustrated*, July 18, 1984, p. 5.

44 . Charles A. Bucher, "Let's Put More Sportsmanship into the Olympics," *Reader's Digest*, September 1955, p. 73.

45. Quoted in Kieran and Daley, *The Story of the Olympic Games*, p. 282.

46. Quoted in Wallechinsky, *The Complete Book of the Olympics*, p. 241.

47. *Portland Oregonian*, May 12, 1988, quoted in Trager, ed., *Sports in America*, p. 148.

48. *Arizona Republic*, April 22, 1988, quoted in Trager, ed., *Sports in America*, p. 149.

49. "War Threats Mess Up Olympics," *U.S. News & World Report*, November 22, 1956, p. 56.

50. Quoted in Miller, *Behind the Olympic Rings*, p. 88.

51. Jimmy Carter, "Statement from Former U.S. President Jimmy Carter on the 1980 Boycott."

52. Quoted in Miller, *Behind the Olympic Rings*, p. 95.

53. *San Diego Union*, September 16, 1988, quoted in Trager, ed., *Sports in America*, p. 153.

54. Craig Neff, "The U.S. Will Rule the Pool," *Sports Illustrated*, July 18, 1984, pp. 99–100.

55. Black Autonomy News Service, "Boycott of the 2000 Olympic Games in Sydney," http://www.webcom.com/nattyreb/black.autonomy/issue505.html.

56. Quoted in Terry O'Neil, *The Game Behind the Game*. New York: St. Martin's Press, 1989, p. 50.

57. *Dallas Morning News*, September 11, 1988, in Trager, ed., *Sports in America*, p. 152.

58. Quoted in Wallechinsky, *The Complete Book of the Winter Olympics*, p. 118.

59. Quoted in Bucher, "Let's Put More Sportsmanship into the Olympics," p. 75.

60. Wallechinsky, *The Complete Book of the Olympics*, p. 205.

Chapter 3: Commercialism

61. Quoted in Miller, *Behind the Olympic Rings*, p. 214.

62. Quoted in Miller, *Behind the Olympic Rings*, p. 57.

63. Quoted in Wallechinsky, *The Complete Book of the Winter Olympics*, p. 159.

64. Quoted in Wallechinsky, *The Complete Book of the Winter Olympics*, p. 159.

65. Quoted in Leonard Koppett, "Overhaul the Olympics," in Podell, ed., *Sports in America*, p. 151.

66. Koppett, "Overhaul the Olympics," p. 151.

67. Miller, *Behind the Olympic Rings*, p. 139.

68. *Sports Illustrated*, July 18, 1984, p. 1.

69. *Sports Illustrated*, July 18, 1984, p. 71.

70. Bruce Wallace, "The Cheaters of Antiquity," *Maclean's*, July 22, 1996, p. 39.

71. Quoted in Grenier, "Olympic Myths," p. 53.

72. Quoted in Robert Lipsyte, "Olympic Idealism Takes a Station Break," *New York Times*, May 19, 1996.

73. Frank DeFord, "The Money Games," *Newsweek*, August 10, 1992, p. 19.

74. Paul A. Witteman, "Less Wretched Excess, Please," *Time*, August 17, 1992, p. 72.

75. Rosenblatt, "Why We Play These Games," p. 137.

76. *Louisville Courier-Journal and Times*, September 16, 1988, quoted in Trager, ed., *Sports in America*, p. 153.

Chapter 4: Size and Participation

77. E. M. Swift, "Calling Arthur Murray," *Sports Illustrated*, April 29, 1995, p. 72.

78. George Vecsey, "Winter Games Are Bigger, but Are They Better?" *New York Times*, February 22, 1998.

79. Wallechinsky, *The Complete Book of the Winter Olympics*, p. xv.

80. Quoted in Joe Henderson, "Too Much Track," *Runners World*, November 1996, p. 18.

81. David Lawday, "Rethinking the Olympics," *U.S. News & World Report*, August 17, 1992, p. 55.

82. E. M. Swift, "Calling Arthur Murray," p. 72.

83. robmiller97, "I Agree, Curling Shouldn't Be There," Yahoo: Recreation and Sports: Sports: 1998 Winter Games: Curling, message 24, February 13, 1998, http://www.yahoo.com/Recreation/Sports.

84. Quoted in Miller, *Behind the Olympic Rings*, p. 203.

85. Wallechinsky, *The Complete Book of the Olympics*, p. xxiv.

86. Henderson, "Too Much Track," p. 18.

87. Lawday, "Rethinking the Olympics," p. 55.

88. Bryan Anderson, "Letters," *Sports Illustrated*, March 23, 1998, p. 12.

89. Quoted in Miller, *Behind the Olympic Rings*, p. 74.

90. Henderson, "Too Much Track," p. 18.

91. Wallechinsky, *The Complete Book of the Winter Olympics*, p. 168.

92. Quoted in John Howse, "Trying to Prevent a Free Ride," *Maclean's*, June 22, 1987, p. 46.

93. R_I_C_K, "Cheating? No," Yahoo: Recreation and Sports: Sports: 1998 Winter Games: Speed Skating: what do you think of the new "clap" speed skates?, message 69, February 12, 1998, http://www.yahoo.com/Recreation/Sports.

94. Quoted in Howse, "Trying to Prevent a Free Ride," p. 46.

95. Koppett, "Overhaul the Olympics," p. 154.

96. Wallechinsky, *The Complete Book of the Olympics*, p. xxiv.

Chapter 5: Drugs

97. Quoted in Wallechinsky, *The Complete Book of the Olympics*, p. 16.

98. Quoted in Stephen Currie, *Issues in Sports*, San Diego: Lucent Books, 1998, p. 43.

99. Quoted in Tom Donohoe and Neil Johnson, *Foul Play: Drug Abuse in Sports*. Rev. ed. Oxford: Basil Blackwell, 1989, p. 12.

100. Quoted in Daniel Benjamin, "The Shame of the Games," *Time*, October 10, 1988, p. 77.

101. Quoted in John Carey, "The Racers' Edge?" *Newsweek*, January 21, 1985, p. 66.

102. Quoted in Sylvain Blanchard, "Running from the World," *New York Times*, July 28, 1996, section VIII, p. 8.

103. Quoted in Michael Bamberger and Don Yaeger, "Over the Edge," *Sports Illustrated*, April 14, 1997, p. 63.

104. Quoted in Geoffrey Cowley and Martha Brant, "Doped to Perfection," *Newsweek*, July 22, 1996, p. 31.

105. Quoted in Pete Axthelm, "Using Chemistry to Get the Gold," *Newsweek*, July 25, 1988, p. 62.

106. Quoted in Eric Niller, "Athletes Are Finding New Ways to Cheat," *San Diego Union-Tribune*, August 5, 1998, p. E-3.

107. Quoted in Bamberger and Yaeger, "Over the Edge," p. 62.

108. Quoted in Rae Corelli, "The Drug Detectives," *Maclean's*, July 22, 1996, p. 28.

109. Quoted in Bamberger and Yaeger, "Over the Edge," p. 64.

110. Quoted in Cowley and Brant, "Doped to Perfection," p. 66.

111. Quoted in Axthelm, "Using Chemistry to Get the Gold," p. 63.

112. Quoted in Tim Layden, "Paralysis by Urinalysis," *Sports Illustrated*, May 26, 1997, p. 108.

113. Quoted in Reuters, "Australia to Push for Tougher Drug Laws," http://espn.sportszone.com/other/news/980807/00796849.html.

114. Hal Higdon, "Did She or Didn't She?" *Runners World*, January 1989, p. 42.

115. Quoted in Chris Wood, "The Perils of Doping," *Maclean's*, July 27, 1992, p. 49.

116. Quoted in Associated Press, "Two U.S. Track Stars Suspended for Drug Use," *Poughkeepsie (New York) Journal*, July 28, 1998, p. 1C.

117. Quoted in Bamberger and Yaeger, "Over the Edge," p. 66.

118. *New York Times*, "The Olympics' Drug Problem," August 9, 1998, p. 18.

119. Quoted in Bamberger and Yaeger, "Over the Edge," p. 70.

120. Quoted in Bamberger and Yaeger, "Over the Edge," p. 70.

121. Quoted in Associated Press, "Samaranch Wants Clear Definition on Drugs," http://espn.sportszone.com/other/news/980726/00784190.html.

122. Quoted in Reuters, "Australia to Push for Tougher Drug Laws."

123. Quoted in Associated Press, "IOC Head's Drug Comments Draw Angry Reaction," http://espn.sportszone.com/other/news/980727/00785338.html.

124. Quoted in Currie, *Issues in Sports*, p. 46.

Suggestions for Further Reading

Michael Bamberger and Don Yaeger, "Over the Edge," *Sports Illustrated*, April 14, 1997.

Fred Coleman, "Nationalism: When the Cheering Stops," *U.S. News & World Report*, February 28, 1994.

Geoffrey Cowley and Martha Brant, "Doped to Perfection," *Newsweek*, July 22, 1996.

Stephen Currie, *Issues in Sports*. San Diego: Lucent Books, 1998. A thorough look at a number of controversies current in sports. Several of the chapters touch on Olympic issues, most notably the chapter on steroids and other drugs.

Tom Donohoe and Neil Johnson, *Foul Play: Drug Abuse in Sports*. Rev. ed. Oxford: Basil Blackwell, 1989. This book deals with drug use among athletes, including much about Olympic competitors. Though somewhat dated, it provides many interesting anecdotes and figures regarding steroids and the history of Olympic drug use.

Stan Greenberg, ed., *Guinness Book of Olympic Records*. New York: Bantam Books, 1992. A listing of medal winners in all Olympic Games for events as of 1992, along with very brief commentary about each Olympics.

John Kieran and Arthur Daley, *The Story of the Olympic Games*. Philadelphia: Lippincott, 1961. Authored by two sportswriters, this book covers the Olympics through 1960. The writing style is frequently dated and the American boosterism becomes wearying, but the writers give a you-are-there feeling for the Olympics of the 1940s and 1950s.

Skip Rozin, "Steroids: A Spreading Peril," *Business Week*, June 19, 1995.

Gary Smith, "It's Greek to U.S.," *Sports Illustrated*, July 29, 1996.

Oliver Trager, ed., *Sports in America: Paradise Lost?* New York: Facts On File, 1990. A collection of editorials from U.S. and Canadian newspapers regarding sports. Includes several on the 1988 Olympics and various Olympic issues.

David Wallechinsky, *The Complete Book of the Olympics.* Woodstock, NY: Overlook Press, 1996. This is indeed the complete book (although this edition does not include the 1996 Atlanta Games). Discusses every event and its history, giving the top eight finishers in each since the opening of the Games. There are anecdotes scattered throughout, some involving the controversies discussed in this book.

———, *The Complete Book of the Winter Olympics 1998.* Woodstock, NY: Overlook Press, 1998. The Winter Games companion to Wallechinsky's Summer Games book; includes the top eight finishers for nearly all events through 1994, along with descriptions of the competitions and the controversies involved.

Works Consulted

Books

Duff Hart-Davis, *Hitler's Games*. New York: Harper & Row, 1986. A careful study of the 1936 Olympics, including the controversies over who should participate and the political dimensions of the Games.

Richard D. Mandell, *The First Modern Olympics*. Berkeley, CA: University Press of California, 1976. A discussion of the Athens Olympics and the beginning of the modern Olympic movement. Also provides plenty of information about the Games of ancient times.

Geoffrey Miller, *Behind the Olympic Rings*. Lynn, MA: H. O. Zimman, 1976. Miller was a journalist who covered the IOC during the 1960s and 1970s. The book's main value is in presenting an as-it-happens account of the controversies and issues of the time: the 1976 boycott by African nations, the rise of professionalism, and the beginnings of commercialization among them.

Terry O'Neil, *The Game Behind the Game*. New York: St. Martin's Press, 1989. Primarily about televised sports during the 1970s and 1980s (O'Neil worked as a producer for CBS), the book includes some interesting firsthand information about the 1972 Olympics and its political controversies.

Janet Podell, ed., *Sports in America*. New York: H. W. Wilson, 1986. A collection of readings on sports in general, including four specifically about the Olympics, with emphasis on the 1984 Los Angeles Games, and another on steroids.

Randy Roberts and James S. Olson, *Winning Is the Only Thing*. Baltimore: Johns Hopkins University Press, 1989. A book discussing some of the things the authors feel are wrong with sports today. Steroid use is among the central focuses.

Periodicals and On-line Sources

Roger Angell, "Gold, Silver, Bronze, Irony." *New Yorker*, July 22, 1996.

Associated Press, "IOC Head's Drug Comments Draw Angry Reaction," http://espn.sportszone.com/other/news/980727/00785338.html.

———, "Samaranch Wants Clear Definition on Drugs," http://espn.sportszone.com/other/news/980726/00784190.html.

———, "Two U.S. Track Stars Suspended for Drug Use," *Poughkeepsie (New York) Journal*, July 28, 1998.

Pete Axthelm, "Using Chemistry to Get the Gold," *Newsweek*, July 25, 1988.

Daniel Benjamin, "Pro vs. Amateur," *Time*, July 27, 1992.

———, "The Shame of the Games," *Time*, October 10, 1988.

Ira Berkow, "FINA's Testing Is Marred, Too," *New York Times*, August 9, 1998.

Black Autonomy News Service, "Boycott of the 2000 Olympic Games in Sydney," http://www.webcom.com/nattyreb/black.autonomy/issue505.html.

Sylvain Blanchard, "Ben Johnson on the Record," *Maclean's*, July 29, 1996.

———, "Running from the World," *New York Times*, July 28, 1996.

Joe Bower, "Olympic Wannabes," *Women's Sports and Fitness*, April 1996.

Charles A. Bucher, "Let's Put More Sportsmanship into the Olympics," *Reader's Digest*, September 1955.

Tom Callahan, "A Clear Victory for Commerce," *U.S. News & World Report*, August 17, 1992.

John Carey, "The Racers' Edge?" *Newsweek*, January 21, 1985.

Kim Carlyle, "Torch Song," *Women's Sports and Fitness*, July/August 1992.

Jimmy Carter, "Statement from Former U.S. President Jimmy Carter on the 1980 Boycott," March 25, 1996, http://www.cc.emory.edu/CARTER_CENTER/RLS96/olym 1980.htm.

Rae Corelli, "The Drug Detectives," *Maclean's*, July 22, 1996.

David Cort, "The Hungarian Olympics," *Nation*, November 24, 1956.

———, "The Myth of the Amateur," *Nation*, September 28, 1964.

Frank DeFord, "The Money Games," *Newsweek*, August 10, 1992.

———, "The Real Gold at the Games," *Newsweek*, August 3, 1992.

Joel Drucker, "Get Tennis Out of the Olympics," *Tennis*, July 1996.

Ron Fimrite, "Facing Bear Facts," *Sports Illustrated*, February 4, 1980.

Richard Grenier, "Olympic Myths," *National Review*, July 29, 1996.

Joe Henderson, "Too Much Track," *Runners World*, November 1996.

Hal Higdon, "Did She or Didn't She?" *Runners World*, January 1989.

John Howse, "Trying to Prevent a Free Ride," *Maclean's*, June 22, 1987.

Roger Kahn, "Let's Pull Out of the Olympics," *Saturday Evening Post*, October 10, 1964.

David Kaplan, "A Real World Series," *Newsweek*, July 8, 1996.

David Lawday, "Rethinking the Olympics," *U.S. News & World Report*, August 17, 1992.

Tim Layden, "Paralysis by Urinalysis," *Sports Illustrated*, May 26, 1997.

"Letters" [Bryan Anderson], *Sports Illustrated*, March 23, 1998.

Robert Lipsyte, "Olympic Idealism Takes a Station Break," *New York Times*, May 19, 1996.

Jere Longman, "Amateur or Pro? Skating Tries Compromise," *New York Times*, August 2, 1998.

———, "DeBruin, Irish Olympian, Is Facing New Questions," *New York Times*, April 30, 1998.

Frank McCoy, "Should the Chariots of Fire Be for Hire?" *Business Week*, September 26, 1988.

Kenny Moore, "The Pawns Make a Move," *Sports Illustrated*, February 4, 1980.

Craig Neff, "The U.S. Will Rule the Pool," *Sports Illustrated*, July 18, 1984.

New York Times, "The Olympics' Drug Problem," August 9, 1998.

New York Times Forums, www.nytimes.com.

Eric Niller, "Athletes Are Finding New Ways to Cheat," *San Diego Union-Tribune*, August 5, 1998.

"The Olympic Century," *Scholastic Update Teachers Edition*, April 12, 1996.

Bob Ottum, "Only You, Mary Lou," *Sports Illustrated*, July 18, 1984.

People Online's Olympic Heroes, "Sebastian Coe," http://www.pathfinder.com/people/sp/olympics/coe.html.

Reuters, "Australia to Push for Tougher Drug Laws," http://espn.sportszone.com/other/news/980807/00796849.html.

Felix Rosenthal, "Warm Days in Moscow," *Sports Illustrated*, February 4, 1980.

Gary Smith, "There's Gold on His Menu," *Sports Illustrated*, July 18, 1984.

E. M. Swift, "Calling Arthur Murray," *Sports Illustrated*, April 29, 1995.

George Vecsey, "Winter Games Are Bigger, but Are They Better?" *New York Times*, February 22, 1998.

Bruce Wallace, "The Cheaters of Antiquity," *Maclean's*, July 22, 1996.

"Wall of Silence May Crumble," *Sports Illustrated*, March 23, 1998.

"War Threats Mess Up Olympics," *U.S. News & World Report*, November 22, 1956.

Paul A. Witteman, "Less Wretched Excess, Please," *Time*, August 17, 1992.

Chris Wood, "The Perils of Doping," *Maclean's*, July 27, 1992.

Yahoo: Sports and Recreation: Sports: 1998 Winter Games, http://www.yahoo.com/Recreation/Sports

Fred Zahradnik, "The Pro Invasion," *Bicycling*, June 1996.

Web Resources

http://olympics.tufts.edu

Information on the ancient and modern Olympic Games, the differences and the similarities, and links to other pages of interest.

http://www.olympic.org

The official site of the IOC and the Games. Includes a lot of information on past and present Games; however, the site is not very user-friendly, and the information can be difficult to locate and access.

http://www.olympic-usa.org

The official site of the USOC. Informative; plenty of information on training sites and athletes, and links to other related sites.

http://www.andrew.cmu.edu/~mmdg/Almanac

These pages give historical information on the Games. Not an official Olympics site, but lots of data on nations, athletes, medal winners, events, and interesting trivia such as lists of all the cities that bid for a particular Games.

http://www.sydney.olympic.org/

The official site for the organizers of the Sydney, Australia, Games to be held in the fall of 2000.

http://headlines.yahoo.com/Full_Coverage/aunz/2000_sydney_olympics/

News, articles, and links relating to the Sydney Games. Some of the articles relate to controversies discussed in this book.

http://cnnsi.com/olympics/

A sports site with extensive Olympic coverage on this page. Includes message boards and links along with news articles.

Index

Picture Credits

About the Author

Stephen Currie is the author of more than thirty books and many magazine articles. Among his nonfiction titles are *Music in the Civil War, Birthday a Day, Problem Play, We Have Marched Together: The Working Children's Crusade,* and *Life in a Wild West Show.* He is also a first and second grade teacher. He lives in upstate New York with his wife, Amity, and two children, Irene and Nicholas.